RETRACING
REALITY

RETRACING REALITY

A *Philosophical Itinerary*

MARIE-DOMINIQUE PHILIPPE

Translated by
The Brothers of St John

t&t clark

Published by T&T Clark
A Continuum imprint
The Tower Building, 11 York Road, London, SE1 7NX
80 Maiden Lane, Suite 704, New York, NY 10038

First published 1999
Reprinted 2006, 2008

ISBN 978 0 567 08664 8 (HB)
ISBN 978 0 567 08710 2 (PB)

British Library Cataloguing-in-Publication Data
A catalogue record for this book is available from the British Library

Typeset by Fakenham Photosetting Limited
Printed and bound in Great Britain by CPI Antony Rowe, Chippenham, Wiltshire

CONTENTS

LETTER TO A FRIEND[1]

My dear friend,

I know how dangerous it is to claim to present the major stages of philosophical inquiry in roughly one hundred and fifty pages, especially in the twentieth century where we are so accustomed to philosophizing by means of dialogue with other philosophers; that is, by situating our thought with respect to theirs, be it in agreement or disagreement. Such an approach, however, interesting as it may be, is not the one I have chosen. Dialogue with other philosophers is only a disposition to true philosophical inquiry which requires returning to the immediate experience of existent realities.

Nevertheless, this return to experience constantly requires purification. Such purification comes about slowly. Our intellect, in its life, is, as it were, 'entangled' in imaginary things, and only with difficulty attains to reality in its 'untamed' and native state.

Hence it seemed good to me – and it is indeed what you asked of me – to present a sort of itinerary specifying the major stages of philosophical reflection, following an order of research (Aristotle would say: according to the 'genetic' order, or an order of generation). I know that I risk all sorts of criticism in doing this, but what would I not do for a friend, who, in reading this book with the desire to seek truth, will understand, thanks to the bond of friendship, everything that can remain implicit and virtual in such a summary? Let nobody claim that we are thus falling into affective subjectivity, reserving the intelligibility of this itinerary for a select few. In reality, what unites us and what constitutes our friendship is the search for truth. I am writing this book for someone who, in seeking truth, is a friend, a philosopher friend, and wishes to be so even more. Therefore, this itinerary, although presupposing a friendly understanding, remains a philosophical itinerary, for it is determined by reality itself – which everyone can experience.

M.-D. Philippe

1 Whose request for a philosophical itinerary was the impetus for the writing of this book.

INTRODUCTION

The search for 'wisdom of life' has always been difficult and rare. Because of his complexity and richness, man[1] always risks being distracted, getting lost in immediate problems and forgetting that which is essential, forgetting that for which he is made, and thereby losing sight of the deeper meaning of his life.

This search for wisdom has become particularly difficult in our time. The cultural milieu in which contemporary man lives does not favor it. The search for such wisdom is considered useless, senseless nostalgia and completely outdated. Indeed, contemporary man's cultural milieu is wholly oriented toward the development of science and technology. We consider efficiency above all else, and often risk forgetting man in his profound destiny. Certainly the development of science and technology affords man new, even surprising, possibilities as regards his power to transform and use matter, his dominion over the physical and biological universe. But does not this prodigious and rapid development often become a sort of excrescence that unbalances man in his human life and suppresses his deep harmony? For this development to be assumed and 'humanized,' would require of man a 'supplement of soul' (to use Bergson's expression), that is, new capacities for loving, thinking, and contemplating. Then this development could truly be at the service of the human person instead of enslaving him and 'materializing' him as it often risks doing. For as soon as this development becomes man's predominant and paramount (if not exclusive) preoccupation, it overcomes and enslaves him. By imposing itself as the essential thing in human life, does it not inevitably engender a certain skepticism regarding philosophy, and especially regarding first philosophy (the philosophy of being, metaphysics)? Indeed, thanks to this development, the 'facade' of our universe is being transformed so quickly that we might be tempted to adopt Heraclitus'

---

1 With all the difficulty and equivocity that the term *man* implies, we maintain it for two reasons: 1) the concreteness and greater richness that it has hitherto implied, as opposed to the terms 'human' or 'human being'; 2) the term *person* has a very specific meaning, as will be shown in the chapter on Metaphysics. We have used it in a very general sense as well, but have sought to respect the specificity of a term that has been transmitted to us. Though not measured by it, philosophy respects the patrimony of thought and language that precedes it. The English language unfortunately does not grant the same distinctions as Latin, for example (*homo* – man; *vir* – man; *mulier* – woman). [-Trans.]

1

assertion: 'Everything changes, everything is relative.' In such a climate of incessant, very tangible transformation, it is difficult to discover in human reality anything other than that which is subject to change, that which is relative. It is very difficult to discern that, at its root, the human intellect is made to go beyond such scientific and technical knowledge, to discover truth of another sort. In short, it is difficult to discern that the human intellect, where it is most 'itself,' is made to attain to that-which-is,[2] existent (or existing) reality in all its depth. It is also difficult to discern that the human intellect can thereby discover, in a more radical and ultimate fashion, what man is: a spirit bound to a body, to the sensible world and, at the same time, capable of transcending it because he has a personal destiny of his own.

Moreover, ideologies of progress, Hegelian dialectic, Marxist dialectical materialism, and Freudian psychoanalytic method have so directly and forcefully marked modern man's sensitivity and imagination that any search for true wisdom seems superfluous and impossible, to be condemned from the outset.

Today it is evident to all that everything is destabilized and called into question at every level. Consequently, we can ask: are we witnessing the end of one world and the birth of a new one? Or are we witnessing *the* end of our universe? We cannot know; but what seems certain (and many are convinced of it) is that the various changes we are observing today – economic changes linked to technical ones which, in turn, are rooted in accelerated scientific progress – necessarily result in a transformation of the social milieu in which man lives and grows. And in this climate, many people, would-be prophets, claim that we are witnessing the birth of a new type of man, we are faced with a new way of thinking and living. In the name of the various transformations of human conditioning (transformations that are intensifying and precipitating themselves with great acceleration), some declare that man is not the same being today as he was in the Middle Ages, the time of Christ, or the time of Aristotle or Socrates. Some claim that 'modern man' must be understood for himself in his 'modernity' – a position that often considers man only at the different levels of his conditioning, that is, at the levels of his becoming.[3] Indeed, today man is often viewed only at the level of his becoming. A psycho-sociological anthropology is thus elaborated which claims to be both exhaustive and philosophical. Man, in his proper reality, is considered only in his

---

2 What exists, reality in so far as it exists, reality in its existence. [-Trans.]

3 The 'process' in which some sort of change comes about in a reality, i.e. the passage to a different form or state either in place, quality or quantity. [-Trans.]

psychological and sociological aspects. Thus, in the name of a psycho-sociological anthropology which considers only man's behavior and 'existential situation,' the philosophy of reality (beyond the psychological and sociological aspects) is rejected; and the metaphysics of that-which-is, considered from the point of view of *being*, is deemed outdated. It is forgotten that the philosophy of that-which-is allows us to discover the various levels of man's life. It allows us to discover his complexity, his true person, his substantial autonomy in being and his orientation towards a personal good. And it allows us to discover his spiritual dimension, a dimension which remains veiled as long as he is considered only in his conditioning and his psycho-social behavior.[4]

We should distinguish between that which stems from economic, political, scientific, and technical transformation (transformation that is a fact and is neither good nor bad in itself) and the various ideologies born in this climate, and yet distinct from it. All of them imply a conception of man, his person, his destiny.

We are often confronted today with a terrible confusion of the evident *fact* of this economic, technical, and scientific transformation of the human community, and a *value judgment* about man and his destiny, a judgment that implies a more or less explicit philosophical vision. From economic, scientific, and social transformation we pass to a complete transformation of man in his most profound aspect; and man is thereby turned into a robot, a cog in the wheel of economic development, of cosmic transformation.

Such confusion did not come about suddenly. It is the fruit of idealistic philosophies, of the ideologies issued from Hegelian philosophy.

Today we are rightly concerned with the pollution of the air, the sea, and the earth, and we are becoming conscious of the urgency of this problem (the biological survival of the human species is indeed at stake). If we were more lucid, we would be more deeply worried about the pollution of the cultural environment in which young people must develop their minds and hearts. For if the pollution of the biological environment can favor the formation of various types of cancer, for example, the pollution of the cultural environment can favor the birth of all sorts of false ideologies, an evil even more frightening for the development of the human mind and heart.

---

4 What is true of philosophy is also true of theology today. There is a current tendency to wish to elaborate a theology using a psycho-sociological anthropology. Here again the 'modernity' of the human person overrides his true spiritual dimension: his capacity to discover transcendent Reality.

Before this danger, we cannot remain indifferent. Neutrality is not possible, for neutrality is already a type of compromise. Is not our intellect made to discover truth? Is not our heart primarily made to love a human person, to love him or her as a friend? No longer fighting for the conquest of truth and no longer seeking friendship between human persons – indeed, considering both impossible – is the result of skepticism and despair.

When threatened with danger, a normal person seeks to fortify himself in order to battle, and save himself and those close to him. We have no right to let ourselves sink without fighting with all our might to save our spirit, i.e., our capacity to reach truth and to love, and to save the minds and hearts of those who are to follow us, our 'cadets' in humanity.

We are, in fact, in a very privileged position for renewing this search for truth. We have sunk very low, and if we are in the 'trough of the wave' we can hardly sink much further. When we consider the various ideologies that have arisen during the last hundred years, and when we look at one of the latest of these, analytic philosophy, we have to recognize that metaphysics has been reduced to nothingness. Not only is the existence of God rejected, but man himself, what he is as a person at the core of his being, is no longer considered. We can hardly go further in abandoning the deep meaning of philosophy. Has not philosophy always been at the service of man? Has it not always allowed him to discover his true end, or finality? In analytic philosophy man disappears; his works and his effects are no longer considered as *man*'s effects, but in themselves, as facts, data whose consequences and antecedents are to be grasped.

As Heidegger loved to quote Hölderlin: 'Where there is danger, there always arises that which saves.' Is not the moment of greatest degradation the closest to a new *élan*? Does not every resurrection require a corpse? For a corpse to resurrect, however, a new spirit is needed to restore it to new life. Our obligation is to do our utmost to provide this new spirit, to restore the human intellect to its true life, to renew it in its most profound and most radical aspect – in its first breath, so to speak.

I know that some will object that to return to metaphysics is to return to the past, to be fixed in immobility, isolated from the modern world, and set outside evolution, for metaphysics immediately places us beyond the directly observable and measurable. But if we understand what realistic philosophy is (and, at its summit, the metaphysics of that-which-is), these objections vanish because, as we shall see, the starting point for realistic philosophy is our experience of the actual, real world, of man as he is in all his dimensions. True philosophy and true metaphysics do not remain in the realm of ideas and immutable principles. They seek to know reality, to know existent man as he is in his complexity as a living being and in his unity of being and spirit. Philosophy cannot be satisfied with describing what is seen and noticed. It cannot be satisfied with measuring observable reality. It seeks (and this is its proper task) to analyze an experienced reality and grasp it in all its dimensions. It especially seeks to know man, who is not and cannot be a 'one-dimensional being.' This is what I would like to show – going beyond the objections, which stem from ideologies which, no longer distinguishing between *idea* and *reality*, cannot know real, existent man as he is. They relativize him in reference to an a priori.[5]

---

5 Though an adjective, 'a priori' has also been used throughout as a noun to designate anything prior to experience which influences in such a way that it reduces its objectivity; commonly referred to as a preconceived notion, but can also be of the affective realm, e.g. emotions which distort understanding. [-Trans.]

1

THE STARTING POINT FOR PHILOSOPHICAL RESEARCH

If the renewal of philosophical research in our time needs to be undertaken in a radical fashion, it is not enough to 'patch up' or complete an already existent philosophy by integrating certain current problems. Indeed, it is as if the mind itself has been 'broken.' The primacy of negation today is such that the intellect, at its root, in its very relation to being, is truly broken. Consequently, it is first necessary to rediscover the starting point for philosophical research beyond this rupture.

If we consider the different Western philosophies, we notice that their starting points are not always the same. For some philosophers the starting point is experience, understood in a very precise sense: the intellect, present to the activities of the senses, judges[1] the existence of the sensed realities; 'this exists,' 'this is.' Is not this the position of the first 'physicists' and, in part, of Heraclitus and those who first consider the universe (the 'empiricists')? It is most clearly the position of Aristotle and, in his footsteps, Thomas Aquinas.

For others, the starting point is the interior experience of the soul, the knowledge that is currently being experienced. In this is discovered interiority, the spiritual life. This position is partially that of Plato. It is especially that of Plotinus, Saint Augustine, and many contemporary philosophers called 'existentialists.'

For yet others, the starting point is consciousness, or reflection upon the act of thinking, *cogito*. Are we not most certain of this? Is it not this that is most immediately grasped? It would seem, then, that philosophical inquiry ought to be elaborated from here . . . This position is that of Ockham, Descartes, and contemporary phenomenologists.

For yet others, the starting point for philosophical research is inspiration, or poetic intuition, which allows the discovery of the invisible present beyond the visible. The fruit of such poetic intuition

---

1 Or discerns.

is what we call 'innate ideas.' These innate ideas, rooted in the mind, permit the discovery of being, beyond the conditioning of becoming. Parmenides is perhaps the first philosopher of intuition; for him it takes on the mode of a 'revelation.' With Plato it is expressed in the reminiscence of ideal Forms, and with Malebranche in innate ideas. We again find philosophical intuition with Bergson, but for him it is more subjective, no longer a question of 'ideal Forms' or of 'innate ideas.' Bergson speaks of the 'intuition of duration.'

Finally, for others, philosophical research begins with the opinions of others. They gather what others say concerning various questions, and seek to make them more precise by confronting the various opinions. This is indeed an interesting and skillful way to philosophize – an elegant and rhetorical way – for it uses the 'sketches' of those who philosophized before, sketches that need to be surpassed. It is very often – alas – the philosophy of 'professors' who, for lack of intuition and experience, rely upon the opinions of others.

There are thus, as it were, five irreducible starting points that are sometimes related or, on the contrary, opposed. It is obvious, however, that these five starting points do not have the same value. It is very important to understand this.

If we wish, therefore, to begin philosophical inquiry, we must first of all know which of these starting points we will use. One might perhaps say that the acceptance of any of these is an a priori choice because it presupposes a determined philosophical perspective. Indeed, should not true philosophy be without any a priori? Does not the philosopher progressively reject all a priori, the better to grasp all that can lead him to truth? Is not an a priori a limitation that encloses us within ourselves and impedes us from listening to others and understanding them, precisely to the extent that they are different and not us?

To avoid any a priori, we must discover the most radical starting point, which imposes itself on our knowledge and excludes any possible choice (choice implies a voluntary aspect and, as such, constitutes an a priori at the level of knowledge). In other words, the starting point for realistic philosophy – for philosophy refusing all a priori – must be the most fundamental, a starting point which, consequently, cannot be contained by the others. Thus, although it neither presupposes nor excludes any of the others, this starting point must situate them in their proper place, according to their proper value. It is proper to philosophical knowledge to be radical and exhaustive. It is proper to philosophical knowledge to be primordial and, at the same time, ultimate, to be knowledge beyond which one cannot go. It therefore corresponds to the deepest exigencies of the human intellect, as intellect.

If we consider the various starting points for Western philosophy in this light, it seems obvious that the starting point can only be experience, experience in the most fundamental sense: the fruit of the alliance between the intellect and the external senses. Such an experience implies a judgment of existence which recognizes that a particular reality exists, that it is, that it imposes itself as a veritable existent reality, not only other than the intellect, but also other than one's own existence. In a judgment of existence, the intellect is capable of recognizing a reality both as existing and able to bring to it a new determination.

This starting point does not exclude internal experience, but it allows us to understand that, interesting as it may be, internal experience is not the first consideration in our searching or inquiry into reality. Internal experience only unveils a certain manner of existing, a relative manner of existing with an 'intentional'[2] mode – whether it is the intentionality of intellectual and sensitive knowledge, passional and volitional affectivity, or the imagination. Indeed, the privilege of interior experience is that it allows us to grasp what we live at the spiritual level: free love (love based upon a choice) for a friend, and intellectual knowledge. What it grants is unique: intimate contact with something spiritual. Hence it so easily seduces us into regarding it as the privileged experience which introduces us into the realm of the spirit; whereas experience through the external senses, which deals with the sensible world, remains bound to material realities. If we seek to know reality where it is most 'itself,' we notice that only experience occurring by means of our external senses allows the judgment of existence to discover an existent reality other than ourselves, and grasp it in its own actual existence. The judgment of existence present in our interior experience does not allow us to discover a reality other than ourselves; it places us in the presence of the real existence of our acts of knowledge and of love, acts which only exist with an intentional mode. Interesting and revealing as they may be, our internal experiences cannot be primary for philosophical research that aims at being thorough. They are certainly closer to 'us' and our reflection, but not to existent reality.

Taking the experience of sensible realities as the primary starting point does not exclude interest in 'consciousness,' but it is no longer considered a starting point. Indeed, in any experience (internal or

2 See below, p. 56 note 4.

external), consciousness is awakened and can be considered for itself. But in so doing, we forget its source. There is consciousness only when we experience existing realities external to us or realities immanent to us, i.e., our own activities. We are conscious of what we live. This consciousness is essential to human life, but it is not primary. Although it is what we most clearly and lucidly grasp, it cannot be the starting point for philosophical inquiry. If we take it as a starting point, the content of our experiences, precisely in so far as it surpasses and escapes us, is laid aside. We enclose ourselves in what is most connatural to us and closest to our human activities. We remain in the immanence of what we are living, or have lived, and can no longer get beyond it. That which is prior to this consciousness is, as it were, forgotten or laid aside.

As for inspiration and intuition, they are not rejected but simply relativized with respect to external experience. For while the latter confronts us with that-which-is, that which imposes itself on us as other than ourselves, inspiration, which comes from us, places us in the presence of 'possible' realities which exist in an 'intentional' manner. The same holds true for intuition, but in a different way. Intuition reveals a new form, a new relation. It does not directly consider that-which-is, and so cannot be the starting point of a philosophy which seeks to grasp what is most fundamental in reality. The starting point in art is the possible (or possibility).[3] Art realizes, or 'brings into being', this or that possible by 'incarnating' it. Philosophy starts with that-which-is. One does not elaborate a philosophy of the possible but of man who is, and of all that is relative to man.

Similarly, mathematics primarily considers possibles, connections, and relations (hence a relationship between mathematics and art). Philosophy cannot consider these first. If and when philosophy considers them, it is always done relative to that-which-is, to existent man considered in himself.

We understand then that a philosophy which rests upon inspiration and intuition, considering them as its starting point, can never be clearly distinguished from art and/or mathematics. It remains a philosophy in which the possible and relation are primary. This is what characterizes idealistic philosophies; idealism considers the possible as the primary aspect of reality (the concrete which exists is only a form of the possible, a realization limiting this possible, in short, an application or 'position').

---

3 Used occasionally as a noun because it has a slightly more concrete character than 'possibility'; indeed, it designates a potential reality and not simply circumstantial potentiality. [-Trans.]

Finally, it is clear that the opinions of other philosophers cannot serve as the starting point for philosophical inquiry into that-which-is. These opinions are not what exists, what primarily is. They are the fruit of human reflection. Yet such opinions must not be systematically rejected as useless. The philosopher cannot be uninterested in what other philosophers and persons have said before him about the reality he seeks to understand. Indeed, either they have reached truth, and he must then recognize it and make use of it in order to discover this truth anew and confirm it himself; or they have been mistaken and have erred, and it is then interesting for him to grasp why they did not reach truth. He must use what they have said in order to avoid making the same mistakes, and to critique their views.

When treating an important subject, the opinions of other philosophers are helpful. By manifesting a problem's difficulty, these often diverse opinions help to find its 'heart.' These opinions can be used to sharpen the intellect and help us to see the complexity of the problem.

In summary, we can say that the starting point for realistic philosophy – one which, from the outset, rejects all a priori – can only be experience in the strongest sense, i.e., experience which involves a judgment of the existence of another existent reality. This does not mean, however, that the other sources of knowledge are excluded; they are simply relativized.

2

QUESTIONING AND EXPERIENCE

Experience lies at the root of admiration, for experience places us in the presence of a reality other than ourselves which possesses something that our intellect does not perfectly grasp. The reality we discover has something that surpasses us. That is why, although we do grasp something of the reality, we are also ignorant of what it is at a deeper level. Doubtless we can say, for example, that such-and-such reality is a dog; but we also know that we do not know the more profound reality of the splendid dog we behold, in other words, what it is. Hence a reality that we experience can awaken in us an admiration which fixes our attention and prevents us from going on our merry way, as we do when we merely use the reality without considering it for itself. Indeed, admiration not only keeps the intellect focused upon that which is experienced, it also prevents the intellect from limiting itself to that which is immediately given in experience. It senses, 'guesses', that the immediate 'datum' is not the reality in its fullness, and that it even risks hiding what is deepest in the reality. We could almost say that, thanks to admiration, the intellect is awakened in a new way, that it has the intuition, as it were, that 'that-which-is', precisely in so far as it is, cannot be reduced to the various data which are immediately grasped (and which are schematized in 'categories').[1] To borrow an image from Plato, we could say that admiration 'raises' our intellect before the experienced reality like a hunting dog before game hidden in the thicket. That is why admiration normally gives rise to questioning.

In questioning, the intellect seeks to grasp what the experienced reality is. It wants to know more profoundly. Questioning is the intellect momentarily distancing itself from the experienced reality in order to grasp it better, to understand it better. It is the intellect manifesting its desire and appetite for knowing. It is like a taut bow ready to send its arrow and to cast its merciless gaze, a gaze which seeks to expose the

1 The various determinations, or modes of being, that can be found in the human person; Aristotle lists ten of them: first substance (the particular individual – Peter, for example), second substance (the fundamental intelligibility – man), quality, quantity, relation, action, passion, time, place, and belongings. [-Trans.]

complexity of the experienced reality and analyze it in order to grasp it better. An intellect that no longer questions can no longer progress. It has reached its peak. Merleau-Ponty once said that an idealist no longer questions. We could say that a dialectical intellect no longer questions but tries to reduce reality to what it grasps of it, while forsaking what it does not understand. An intellect that questions, on the contrary, hungers for progress. It wants to advance, to probe more deeply ... nothing can stop it. Here again, it is like the hunting dog who, watchful before the hidden game, wants to draw it out. Questioning is to the philosopher what hypothesis is to the scientist. In fact, a question is a sort of radical, fundamental hypothesis, a hypothesis in its most elementary form which expresses simply and exclusively the natural appetite of the intellect for penetrating further into existent reality, but without the 'possible' character we see in scientific hypothesis. In questioning there is a direct dialogue between the intellect and existent reality.

There are, in fact, different fundamental questions which indicate the various paths of research for our intellect hungering for discovery. Following Socrates, the great philosopher of question, Aristotle specified the various forms of question and their irreducible structures. As soon as it has recognized that a particular reality exists, the intellect immediately seeks to know *what it is*. Thanks to the orientation of this question, it discovers the determination of a reality, its proper intelligibility, form, difference, that whereby it is distinguished from other realities. The intellect then questions to know *what* the reality *is made of*. In this way, it seeks to discover the matter in which the form is realized. These questions are very explicit when looking at a work of art, a tool, a machine: What is its matter? Wood, steel, nylon ...?

The intellect also asks *whence* this reality *comes:* What is its origin? Is it close or far? Who made it? The intellect finally asks: *For the sake of what* does this reality exist? Is it a tool to be used? Is it something natural? Is it a person we consider and seek to know for his or her own sake? The intellect can also ask *based on what model* the reality has been made. It can seek out its prototype in order to understand it better and grasp the exemplariness of its form.

Is this sufficient, however? The intellect can also ask *how* this reality is, how it was made, how it can be preserved, how it decays, how it can be modified, completed, utilized, dominated, etc. The question of 'how,' as can be seen, is secondary in comparison with the preceding ones, and a perfect response is only possible by presupposing the answers to them (in fact, we must admit that we often want to answer the 'how' question immediately, thereby remaining at the level of conditioning and phenomenon).

In the practical order of prudential action and artistic and technical realization – of 'acting' (*agere*) and 'making' (*facere*) – we must also specify *place* and *time* (situation and occasion). When must one act? Do we have this or that place to act? Are we in an appropriate situation? Is it the right moment? The circumstances of time and place are of paramount importance in order for human action to succeed and be perfectly efficient. The questions of number, size, and speed are also important (consider, for example, the economy and defense), for number can so profoundly transform the conditioning of an action that it seems to modify its nature. From a philosophical perspective, however, these questions are obviously secondary (except, of course, in a dialectical perspective).

At a deeper level, the first five questions (What is it? What is it made of? Whence does it come? For the sake of what is it? Based upon what model has it been made?) are the most important ones in philosophical inquiry. They are the most fundamental, those which arise in the presence of an existent reality. The order of these questions varies, but they always recur; we cannot avoid them. The question of 'how' is equally essential, but it is only asked secondarily – at least as regards philosophical knowledge. As regards realization and efficiency, 'how' becomes primary – and also perhaps as regards scientific knowledge. We are touching here on an extremely important problem which must be analyzed in order to understand better the difference between a philosopher's path and that of a scientist. Is not a philosopher, above all, a person of the first five questions, a person of 'why'? Is not a scientist, above all, a person of 'how,' especially when scientific knowledge is used for technical purposes?

Given the importance of questioning for a realistic philosopher – because it indicates the paths to be followed – we must pursue the analysis further. Can we say (independently of Aristotle's authority) that these five major questions impose themselves on us? And must we say, because of this, that there cannot be any others, and that any budding philosopher must necessarily consider all of them?

Our intellect only reaches (the) reality where it is most itself by means of our senses. The judgment of existence arises from an alliance between our intellect and our external senses. This being so, contact between our intellect and 'that-which-is' occurs in five different ways. There are, as it were, five fundamental determinations of our intellect (we could say five fundamental 'pleats' or 'grooves') by which the intellect can question, and so return to the experienced realities in order to discover in them something other than the immediately given – a passage from the *existential* to the *existentiale*. These five fundamental determinations both orientate our intellect and allow it to surpass the immediate data of our experiences. Linked to *sight*, the intellect seeks to specify the determination of the seen reality: what it is. Linked to *touch*, it seeks to detect what is absolutely fundamental in the touched reality: what it is made of. Linked to *hearing*, it seeks to grasp the origin of the reality experienced through sound or noise: whence it comes. Linked to *smell*, the intellect seeks to grasp the reality which attracts by its scent: what it exists for. Linked to *taste*, it seeks to discover the model of the reality grasped in its distinctive flavor.

It is true that we do not immediately discern these secret and profound connections, for we are far from our primary, utterly qualitative experiences. We think more from our imaginative representations than from our sensations. We are always somewhat afraid of our sensations. After all, can they not deceive us? It is obvious they can, but this is hardly reason enough not to make use of them. Fear is often a poor adviser! We must, on the contrary, be all the more vigilant and attentive to the originality of these alliances between the intellect and sight, between the intellect and touch. We then discover these orientations or 'calls' which become questions.

These connections also involve the imagination, which is between sensation and intellect. By it and in it, sensations are united into an 'image' which represents the reality that is experienced. An image draws the diversity of these contacts into a certain unity, which explains why the diversity of questions is easily reduced to the sole question of 'how'. Indeed, an image only gives rise to a single question in our intellect: how – the composition or the division of the various elements which an image synthesizes or opposes. That is why, to the extent to which the image replaces the various sensations, only one question remains: how?

Questioning in these various ways, the intellect returns to the experienced reality to discover in it what it was seeking. Here we are in the presence of a very particular cooperation between the questioning intellect and the experienced reality. This cooperation leads to and brings about what is called an 'induction,' that is, the discovery of a proper principle and a proper cause. To each of these questions there corresponds a special induction, the discovery of a proper principle. The first philosophical analysis of an experienced reality is done in this way. By thus analyzing what is deepest in an experienced reality, the intellect grasps what it is (its determination), what it is made of (its matter), whence it comes (its origin), and for the sake of what it is (its end). These inductions are indeed a passage from the visible to the invisible. It is by and through them that the intellect discovers its proper good, that which perfects it. Consequently, the true quality of an intellect is manifested in its capacity to induce, to discover the proper principles of an experienced reality, much more than in its aptitude for deduction.

After the discovery of these principles, the intellect returns to the experienced reality and considers it in this new light, that of its proper principles, in order to discover how these principles occur in the reality, their manner of existing. It is then that the intellect can deduce the properties of the reality and perfectly know it, i.e., in and through its proper causes. Aristotle called this perfect knowledge 'science'; and for him it constituted philosophical knowledge.

Let us now examine the major experiences of man which will allow us to discover his principles and his proper causes.

The first experience, the one closest to man, the one to which he always returns, is *work* and, parallel to that, is *friendship*. These are the two experiences most connatural to man. The former enables him to grasp that he is a part of the universe, yet capable of modifying it; and the latter, that he can be close to his fellow man and love him, know him (as another self) and live with him.

These two experiences normally lead to a third: man as part of a community, cooperating with others, becoming the source of a common good upon which he also depends. These are the three primary experiences of human life upon which, as we shall see, human philosophy, practical philosophy, is elaborated. This is the basis of all realistic philosophy: man present to and transforming the universe, man present to man and cooperating with him to form a human milieu. We have different philosophical conceptions of man depending upon the order of value we attribute to these three experiences.

But this is not enough. We cannot stop there, for these three experiences presuppose three other, more fundamental ones. The experience of work involves that of matter (that which is capable of being transformed). The experience of friendship involves that of the living being (for a friend can die and my love for him is not the source of his life). The experience of cooperation in building the 'common good' leads us to pose a new question about man's end: can man find his end, his full blossoming as man, in cooperation? Is there not in man's person something greater, more noble, more spiritual than cooperation, which always remains linked to the common good? Who is this human person? How can we grasp his nobility? Is not the human person, in his most 'personal aspect,' ordered to another, absolute, good beyond the human person? Is there an absolute Good? A philosopher must pose this question, for he has no immediate experience of it. Even if religious traditions speak of a Good, he cannot accept these traditions a priori. He must verify that they are well grounded. Thus, from the experience of cooperation and by virtue of the question 'What is man?,' the philosopher is obliged to return to what is common to all experiences, the radical basis of them all, the judgment of existence (in and for itself): 'this is'; and from there pose the question of being: what is being?[2]

Thanks to these last three experiences, we can understand better what man is. We can understand him better as including, by his body, *matter* capable of undergoing the influences of the universe. We can understand him better as the *living being* 'par excellence,' with deep autonomy and capable of organizing and developing himself. We can understand him better as a *person* capable of asking the question, 'Does there exist a transcendent Reality?' and of adoring and contemplating this Reality.

Philosophy seeks to understand as perfectly as possible who man is, and to discern the various orientations possible for him. In addition to this inquiry there is critical reflection. Indeed, philosophy must be lucid about the various paths or developments of its research. It must compare them with those of other philosophies and justify its orientation. Such critical reflection involves the art of *thinking* and *discoursing* (or saying) with rectitude and the greatest logical accuracy. It thereby allows for clearer, more precise communication. There are different ways of saying what we bear within us, what we think. We can say it primarily so that the other person grasps the conceptual content of our thought. In this case, in order that our thought be as exact as possible, it follows that our speech must use logic that is as exact as possible. If, on the contrary, we desire above all to communicate our impressions, what we profoundly feel, our speech must then be poetic. It no longer has recourse to logic, but to the art of poetry.

Let us now examine each of these stages of philosophical inquiry.

2 Here we see the difference between a realistic position and the position of those who claim that the major philosophical question is: 'Why is there being and not nothing?' or, according to the formulation of Leibniz: 'Why is there something instead of nothing?' (Let us also not forget Shakespeare's alternative: 'To be or not to be, that is the question.') This question is understandable at the poetic level where the possible is primary; but, transposed to the philosophical level, it can no longer be primary, at least according to realistic philosophy where the possible can only be understood in the light of act. In a realistic position, the judgment of existence can be brought out in all our experiences, in which it is present, but it is never primary in the order of our research. In a position more or less dependent upon idealism – consciously or not – the 'principle' question is, 'Why is there being and not nothing?'

3

THE PHILOSOPHY OF WORK[1]

There is no need to insist upon the fact of the experience of work. This is certainly the experience had most frequently by the greatest number of persons. It is certainly the one which marks people most and the one by which people best grasp their conditioning, that is, their temporality and dependence upon the universe, as well as their capacity to transform it. This experience seems to be first according to the genetic[2] order. Although natural appetite – that is, instinctive, sensitive, and passional appetite for the mother's milk – is certainly the first manifest vital activity in an infant, this sensible and instinctive appetite is not fully conscious. We cannot consider it, therefore, to be a true experience. Moreover, does this appetite imply a voluntary, spiritual love of the child for its mother, or even for the proper Source of its being? We cannot respond immediately to this question; to give a positive or negative response, without philosophical reflection, would be an a priori. Indeed, an affirmative response would not be the fruit of an immediate sensible experience. It seems, therefore, that the experience of work, the transformation of matter (in the most general sense), is genetically speaking our first experience; for this experience is truly conscious and implies a certain judgment of existence. When a little boy plays with a construction kit, or a little girl with a doll, neither of them is really conscious of what he or she is doing. They are playing and, when playing, they remain in a wonderful, imaginary world. Once school begins, they will have to 'work' and submit to certain rules, and this work will require attentiveness and reflection which awakens a certain consciousness.

If work is really our first conscious experience, this experience conditions all our other experiences and, if we are not careful, can even determine them. For, as we know, that which is first in a given genus conditions everything which follows it. (Is not the first in a series at the head of the line?) All that comes after it is relative to and dependent

1 Cf. also our study *Philosophie de l'art* (2 volumes, Editions Universitaires, Paris, 1991), where the philosophy of *making* is treated from a different perspective.
2 The order of becoming, that is, of the imperfect towards the perfect.

upon it. Very often, everything which follows the first is determined by it (the phenomenon of 'repetition'). If we consider man only in his becoming, in his relation to the physical world, work is no longer simply the first experience genetically, it becomes the predominant experience, that to which all others are referred. This is what happens in political philosophical perspectives which only consider man's collective aspect. If we only consider man's conditioning, this experience is necessarily central.

The experience of work allows us to understand how man dominates matter and how he can transform it. Man acquires a certain knowledge of matter through his work, a knowledge which is relative to the very transformation he brings about. The resulting work is the fruit of man's labor upon matter. The first time man realizes a work, and every time he realizes a new one, is he not surprised by the efficiency of his labor and the resistance or the softness, the malleability, of the matter used? This work is realized by means of his labor and he can admire it; and this astonishment and admiration lead him to ask what this work is of which he is the author.

The work which brings his labor to completion can either be a utilitarian work – a tool, for example, an instrument which allows the worker to labor anew with greater efficiency and rapidity – or a work of art pleasant to behold. A utilitarian work, ordered to a particular usage, possesses a form relative to the person who uses it; whereas a work of art possesses a form of expression capable of attracting our intellect and pleasing it. In a work of art, the form is resplendent; it is perfectly itself. In a utilitarian work, the form is one of adaptation. We see how, by specifying the *form* of the work realized by man's labor, we also discern the *end* for which it is made. Indeed, the work is aimed either at artistic knowledge, or utilization, or greater efficiency. The discovery of the form and the end are simultaneous.

Although what the work *is* is specified by its form, it is also distinguished by its matter, which plays a very important role not only in a work of art, but also in a utilitarian work. It even constitutes one of the proper qualities of such-and-such a work: this tool is steel, this painting is oil, this sculpture is wood, etc.

It is from a work of art that the first distinction between *form* and *matter* is drawn. In analyzing a work of art we first discover its form and its matter. The form is what determines it and gives it its originality. The matter is capable of being transformed and modified, and gives the work of art its foundation, its rooting in the physical world. The matter is what it is made of.

Nevertheless, regarding a work of art, the most important discovery is its immediate source. It comes from man's work; that is obvious. But for work to be truly human, what elements must it imply? Human work takes place in quite varied conditions, which sometimes modify it to such an extent that one wonders whether these conditions have not changed its nature. Thus we need to look at human work in its simplest and most visible realization, that of an artisan, a craftsman. It is here that we can grasp the full range of different types of work.

An artisan's work always presupposes a certain choice, a certain option. Through his work, an artisan makes what he wishes to accomplish: this pair of clogs, this particular table, that particular chair. He chooses the model on which he desires to work. He chooses one material over another for the sake of what he wants to make. He chooses a particular instrument and a particular method, following a plan of realization. If he is truly an artist and has the time and the necessary skill, he can invent his own model, he can 'create' a new style which he can execute. This is the proper causality of artistic activity: exemplary causality (the model after which the work is made).

What is at the origin of this exemplary causality? The question of inspiration and the birth of an artistic 'idea,' a 'model,' arises here. What is inspiration? Where does it come from? It is important to grasp the proper character of inspiration, this special source of a particular type of knowledge. Inspiration is indeed at the root of a new knowledge regarding 'possibles,' that which can be realized by the artist. In this sense, inspiration implies a sort of revelation and illumination. Inspiration, for an artist, is a new way of looking at everything around and within. From this 'vantage point' everything is viewed in a new light, as 'possible' in the sense of 'realizable,' susceptible to being made, to being expressed.

What characterizes this new knowledge coming from the light of inspiration, is precisely that it has to do with 'possibles,' that which can be realized by the artist. The objectivity of such knowledge is therefore completely different from other types of 'objective' knowledge, knowledge which considers such-and-such existent reality. Inspiration itself is the source of these 'possibles.' The inspired intellect of an artist gives itself its own determination, its own specification. It provides itself with the immediate meaning of the possibles it knows – as idealists say of all philosophical knowledge. In other words, if inspiration were the model of all philosophical knowledge, the idealists would be correct; but if inspiration is proper to artistic knowledge, then idealists tend to reduce philosophical knowledge to poetic knowledge.

Inspiration stems from the deep alliance between intellect and imagination. That is why some have spoken of 'creative imagination.' In reality, the intellect is present in the very depths of the activities of our imagination and gives them a new capacity for 'creativity.'[3] This explains why poetic inspiration gives birth to artistic ideas.

Although the work of an artisan who invents his own model involves creative inspiration, the work of a simpler artisan (who does not invent his own model) does not demand it. A model to be reproduced and copied suffices for him. So, is the work of an unskilled laborer, a factory worker, someone who labors on an assembly line, really human work? Human labor calls for completion in a work. Although it requires efficiency, efficiency only has meaning because of the work it produces. Efficiency alone, efficiency for itself, has no meaning. If a worker is only a cog in a complex organization which involves an extreme division of work for greater efficiency, his work no longer has deep meaning for him. Taken to an extreme, in such work man is only an instrument, an anonymous intermediary. Consequently, not only are the phases of inspiration and invention missing, there is no longer even an end. There is no precise goal. The worker is remote-controlled in the name of a project to be completed and a work of whose concrete realization he is totally ignorant. Such work can no longer ennoble man; it can only wear him down.

It would be equally interesting to understand how tools can modify human work. Tools progressively take on a value which increasingly imposes itself, and require considerable investment; eventually they modify human work to its limit, for there comes a point at which the worker is at the service of a tool, a machine, and no longer the reverse. Here again we touch on the destruction of human work. If the working man is placed at the service of a tool, a machine, his work is then completely relative to the pure efficiency of the machine. His work becomes a *sine qua non* condition for efficiency, for the operating capacity of the machine. It is no longer human. Far from ennobling, it degrades, for the working man becomes completely dependent upon the tool (except, of course, when he is the superintendent of the machine. As superintendent, he remains in control of its operation and is thus no longer completely relative to it, although the efficiency is primarily dependent upon the quality of the machine.) This work can

3 Creative imagination, in fact, presupposes a series of experiences which involve external sensation. These experiences are of a particular type which can be called 'sensitive artistic experiences.' Artists are always considered as having special sensitivity, sensitivity which detects qualities which the 'common folk' do not grasp. Think of the way in which a painter considers a landscape or a musician listens to the sounds of the forest ...

become horrible, no longer allowing the working man to experience *human* work. He only experiences his dependence, his slavery to efficiency.

Furthermore, such work, which is entirely at the pace of the machine, can easily cease to be a true cooperation of man with matter via the tool. It is rather an exploitation of matter, an exploitation in which the working man is an unconscious accomplice, because he is only there as a *sine qua non* condition. But sharing, even unconsciously, in such exploitation of matter can only be a source of sadness, breakdown, and disgust. Exhilarating as it is to be source of a great work involving true cooperation with the universe, it is degrading to be someone who powerlessly witnesses the tyrannical exploitation of the universe; instead of 'cultivating' the universe, bringing it to completion, and fulfilling it, man exploits it. He degrades it and empties it of its true grandeur.

Those who philosophize about work must always ask the question: To what extent does contemporary technical work still bring about the cooperation of man with matter? Is it tyrannical exploitation of matter? Is man rendering the world more inhabitable? Or is he, on the contrary, in the process of making it uninhabitable? Does this work permit man to blossom in a vital milieu that is increasingly human? Or is it in the process of destroying man's vital milieu? We must also ask whether work in which man is totally relative to an instrument is not degrading.

If we look only at the efficiency of work, we shall, of course, assert that there is continual progress; but if we consider the fruit of labor and the cooperation of man with matter, it is another story.

A dialectical conception of labor, in the Marxist *praxis* vein, cannot respond to the problem, nor even grasp it; for it never considers a work as the fruit of labor. It only considers the efficiency of the labor transforming matter and transforming the working man. Everything remains in the immanence of *praxis*.

Pure economic liberalism, which also considers only the efficiency of work, cannot consider the problem either, nor understand its significance. To consider the problem, we must look beyond work to the working man, to man as he works.

A philosophy of the working man must allow us to grasp a real dimension of man: man is capable of dominating the universe, transforming and utilizing it by means of tools he makes (from flint to computers). A philosophy of the working man reveals to us a particular type of man and a very special aspect of his freedom. It is clear that work – the cooperation of man with matter (that is, the capacity to be transformed) – develops in man an acute sense of his power, his superiority over everything that is capable of being transformed; and this instills in him an increasingly acute consciousness of his freedom and dignity as *homo faber* who can, if he desires, if it seems good to him, work or not work. Work increases his sense of autonomy, security, and self-esteem. On the other hand, a working man who is reduced to being only the slave of a tool, a machine, experiences a feeling of frustration. Is this not a radical anomaly? Work, which should ennoble man, degrades and damages him. The efficiency of his work no longer belongs to him, because he is himself completely relative to the efficiency of a machine. And if the machine belongs to another, he is, as it were, doubly expropriated from his own work. The ensuing feeling of frustration can drive a working man to a kind of destruction or revolt; it is intolerable to depend on both a machine and the person who owns it.

Let us not forget that work, as we noted at the outset, is our fundamental, radical experience, the one which most profoundly marks our human conditioning and is closest to our psychical consciousness. It is also the experience which gives us the most acute sense of time. The 'becoming' of work can be measured by time, even if its qualitative aspects and essential content escape such measurement. This becoming is essential for work and characterizes its proper conditioning; it is not simply a secondary aspect. That is why, as long as work qualifies and ennobles man, it enables him to blossom. It is part of human growth and keeps him in a state of euphoria. But as soon as work degrades man and stifles him, it becomes intolerable for him. Man can bear it for a while, but he cannot integrate it without destroying himself. Hence, he very quickly rejects it.

If work, which should ennoble, degrades, there was an error or a false orientation at some point. There was progressive deviation. The true end of labor – the work, that for which labor should be – was no longer considered. There was withdrawal into efficiency for its own sake. Tools considered in their efficiency were the only thing considered ... and man was forgotten.

4

THE PHILOSOPHY OF FRIENDSHIP

Important as it may be in human life, work is not man's only experience. There is another fundamental, important experience: friendship[1] wherein man discovers, not matter as in the experience of work, but man himself, one who is similar to him, whom he can consider and love as another self – or, on the other hand, who can become a rival, and even an enemy.

The experience of friendship reveals to me what a friend is: someone who is my personal good, someone who is capable of perfecting me, fulfilling me, revealing to me who I am because he is my friend, because he loves me, and because I am also his personal good.

This experience is not solely an internal experience in the proper sense, nor solely an external experience which involves an alliance with the external senses. Friendship characteristically involves these two types of experience, both internal and external. For the experience of friendship is not only the experience of my love for someone; it is also the experience of the friend. The experience of loving is an interior experience – I am conscious of loving. But the experience of the friend himself, the experience of the other loving me, also requires an external experience. Experiencing a friend entails being conscious of loving, but it does not stop at this consciousness. It goes further. It attains to the other person who loves me, and this requires a judgment of existence.

This experience of my love ('of friendship') for someone who loves me arouses within me a sense of wonder and admiration. It is wonderful to

---

1 We have chosen to use the simple term 'friendship' to translate *l'amour d'amitié*, literally 'love of friendship', an expression used by Thomas Aquinas (Ia IIae Q26 art 4). It is the equivalent of the Greek φιλια *philia*. The word friendship has two connotations in English when used without any modifier. It can mean either 'a relationship wherein one is attached to another through human affection,' or it can mean 'a relationship with an acquaintance, that is, a person whom one knows without being particularly close.' The use of the term friendship here emphasizes the first sense, that is, spiritual love for another, love implying a mutual personal choice. It is distinguished from utilitarian friendship and pleasurable friendship. [-Trans.]

love and be loved precisely by someone whom I love, by someone who awakens love within me, for he is really my good. He is someone thanks to whom my person can blossom.

I can, of course, be content with describing this love and what it does for me, what it awakens in me, and how it fulfills me; but I can also go further and ask: What is this love? What is love?

I must return to the experience of friendship to answer the question; for only this experience allows me to know what love is in the strongest, most intimate, and most personal sense. Indeed, I grasp within me various ways of loving. There is a sensitive, passional, or passionate, love for an immediate, sensible good: I love good wine, I love to look at particular landscapes. There is an instinctive love: I love to drink when I am thirsty. This is a biological need which imperiously and blindly directs us towards something that can satisfy the need, which, once possessed, fulfills a living being in and through a certain enjoyment. This biological need, or instinctive appetite, is often linked to a passional love, for it awakens a sensible appetite in us (of which we are normally conscious). There is also an imaginative, 'romantic' love, which orients us towards a kind of ideal we have formed within ourselves. Finally, there is the awakening in us of a volitional, or voluntary, spiritual love for a personal, spiritual good. This spiritual love awakens in us as a desire; and if this personal good is a friend who loves us, this desire, thanks to reciprocal love, blossoms into deeper love.

This personal, spiritual love does not exclude the other loves. It tends toward assuming them, for a friend can be loved sensitively and instinctively. It can even give rise to a sort of imaginary halo, especially if, after being present, the friend is absent. Indeed, absence favors the development of the imagination, which easily idealizes the one we love. We place him on a pedestal. Nobody is like him. He is unique! If these various inferior loves grow too violent and exclusive, they can become the rival of the spiritual love and even stifle it.

This variety of loves must help us to understand what love is; all of them, in different ways, are 'love.' The object of each is a known good, or at least one considered as such (except instinctive love, which has no need of prior knowledge; instinct suffices). It is precisely this known good which arouses in us a particular kind of love: a passional love if it is a good known by sensation, an imaginative love if it is a good reached by the imagination, a spiritual love if it is a good revealed by the intellect.

But if the diversity of knowledge(s) determines the diversity of love(s), should we not then say that knowledge specifies love? We may be tempted to say so, but this is not exact. In reality it is the known *good* that determines love. It is the good that we love and not our knowledge of it. The knowledge that we have of it is a necessary condition for the birth of love; but the good itself is the source of the love. The good itself arouses love, by drawing to itself. We see this very clearly in the personal love in friendship. By his personal goodness, a friend attracts his friend to himself, arousing love in him. As a result, his friend is united to him and rendered connatural to him.

A friend loves his friend for himself and not because of his qualities. Such qualities may have been the occasion for their mutual love, but they do not specify their love. Love is immediately determined by the friend in his personal goodness; and this goodness is what the friend substantially is, including his qualities and his actual love for his friend. This love finalizes[2] him and gives him his true ultimate goodness. The friend, in his personal goodness, is loved for himself, as a friend.

Thus the love (in friendship) is what inclines a friend towards his friend, what allows him to go beyond himself in order to tend wholly towards the other, his good. Love is 'ecstatic';[3] it draws out of oneself and ordains to the good that attracts and finalizes. This ecstasy obviously does not occur at a substantial, metaphysical level. It occurs at the level of a vital operation, with an intentional mode.

Although love is ecstatic, it also involves a capacity for receiving or welcoming. Although he is completely directed towards his friend, a friend is at the same time completely receptive to him. He receives him into his inmost heart. Although when we love we are completely 'towards' the one we love, the one loved is also in the inmost depths of the one who loves. Ecstasy involves a new interiority, a new capacity for carrying the person we love.

In this sense we can also say that love gives an *élan* and an invincible strength. No longer does the one who loves feel his fatigue, for he is victorious over it. But, at the same time, he is both much more vulnerable and capable of enduring or suffering. He senses his fragility more acutely. We clearly see that the intellect and human language cannot really say what love is, for love does not lend itself to analysis. The only thing that we can say is that love is wholly relative to the known good and unites us to it.

2 'Finalizing' is what a human good – which is a certain absolute – does, i.e., brings to completion, orders what subsequently become secondary goods, and gives meaning. [-Trans.]
3 The Greek term εκσταοις″, used by Aristotle and Plato, conveys a displacement. [-Trans.]

The love in friendship, which is love *for* the friend, is realized in a mutual choice. Friends choose one another as friends. They make a preferential choice of one another that must be conscious. Both of them must be aware of the choice and freely consent to it. Otherwise, it is no longer a choice of love.

In loving one another and choosing one another in their love, friends have the intention of loving one another more and more. Indeed, there are no boundaries in love, for we love a spiritual good which draws us, a human person who, in a certain sense, is an absolute with something infinite. The intention to love increasingly allows for an identity of wills between friends. And so that this identity of wills be always more perfect, friendship requires a communal life and the realization of some common work. Otherwise, it risks losing its realism and becoming idealized.

In reflecting upon the experience of friendship, we discover the characteristic demands of human activity, of moral activity. This is only normal, for moral activity blossoms in a personal relationship and responsibility, and in friendship, personal relationship and responsibility are most perfect and most conscious. Thus friendship allows us to discover fully what moral activity is, as well as its proper demands. Ethical activity, unlike artistic activity, implies at the outset the spiritual love of a personal good. There can be no moral activity as long as this spiritual love does not exist.

This spiritual first love, this profound inclination of our will drawn to a good, that is, to a human person who is our spiritual good, remains something hidden and buried. It is certainly primary but it needs to become more explicit and precise. It is like the 'down filling' in a duvet: it maintains the inner warmth of our heart, but remains hidden, beyond our psychical consciousness.

This spiritual first love needs to be determined by a moral intention. The personal good that is loved then becomes our end. We tend towards it in order to reach and become united with it, for we know that we do not as yet possess it. We love it and we are affectively united with it, yet there is a distance. It is truly the end that we pursue. We seek the person loved to be our friend.

It is important to understand the connection between the known good that arouses love and the end that determines our intention. Only a good can be a true end; but all goods are not ends. In order for a good to be an end which awakens an intention in us, it must be capable of serving as a principle which polarizes a whole series of other, secondary, goods that it relativizes and orders. It is from the love of this good that the intention is born which considers the good as an end, a principle of order with respect to a series of other goods. We know the importance of intention in our moral life. We remain an errant being, capable of all sorts of distractions as long as there is no true life intention, for there is no order in us. Spiritual love alone does not suffice. It must be organized and strengthened; for if it is not organized from within, under the influence of the imagination it will easily be transformed into a whim. If spiritual love is not fortified and ordered by the intellect, which grasps our end in the personal good, that is, the principle of order for our activities, the spiritual love will deteriorate, lose its nobility, and become nothing but a whimsical appeal.

As soon as we have decided to pursue this end, to act so that the person loved be our friend, we then seek means to reach it. We deliberate on various possibilities, on all that might be of help to us. It is then good to seek advice from those more experienced than us, whom we know well and who love us. In this way we can become informed. Then, from among the various means we discover, we choose the one most likely to enable us to attain to the desired end. This choice remains free, for means never impose themselves as necessity. They are often relative in their proximity both to the willed end, and to our abilities. We can, of course, always choose the means closest to us and most adapted to us; or we can choose the most efficient means for attaining the pursued end. Obviously, in certain cases only one means presents itself and, because it imposes itself, can no longer be freely chosen.

Having made this choice, we move to the execution. For this, we must command ourselves: 'Do this.' It is time, the moment is right. Then we 'go for it,' 'take a dive,' and do our best, with the greatest possible diligence and ardor.

It is good to compare the various phases of moral activity with those of artistic activity, for they are always interconnected in our life. Thus we see how philosophers who are more sensitive to artistic efficiency than to end often reduce the philosophical analysis of moral activity to that of artistic activity.

Without developing a full parallelism here, let us briefly suggest or outline it. Moral activity begins with love and comes together in an intention. Artistic activity begins with knowledge – that is, sensible experience and a certain artistic contemplation; it then springs forth, totally renews itself, and comes together in inspiration. Intention is to the moral life what inspiration – the source of every project – is to the artistic life.

The moral intention requires a phase of advice, or counsel, necessary for choice, or election. The advice phase is not required in artistic activity. There, only the creative choice imposes itself, which is a passage from the possible to the necessary. In moral activity the choice continues to be about what is contingent.

Moral choice is followed by a command – an *imperium* – regarding execution, that is, the setting in motion, engaging or exercise of our various spiritual and sensitive powers. If we attain thereby our personal good, we rest in it in joy. In artistic activity, the choice is followed by labor, which is brought to completion in the realization of *a work*. We can stop only when the work has been completed. This realization needs to be constantly monitored by a critical judgment. It requires self-lucidity in order to verify that what is being done corresponds to the initial project. In and of itself, labor has a certain opaqueness, the opaqueness of matter. That is why it requires this critical reflection, which does not exist in the development of execution at the moral level. The act of initial command suffices, for it is itself an act of the practical intellect.

The development of these two activities forms the immediate framework of our human activities. Nevertheless, in each of us, one of these developments is ordinarily more explicit and more actual than the other, and this makes us more sensitive to either immediate efficiency or end. We must be aware of this in order to understand it in others and rectify it in ourselves. Is not this taking charge of oneself? Is not this intelligently taking our various energies and ordering them? If the development of one of these activities were to gain an exclusive upper hand to the detriment of the other, there would be total disequilibrium in human life – which would be horrible.

When man is completely absorbed by *homo faber* and is no longer sensitive to anything but the demands of efficiency, the source of his love very quickly dries up. Efficiency then replaces fruitfulness and the human person is regarded only as matter capable of being transformed or as a tool to be used. There is no longer any respect for the human person. Is this not the great danger in today's world? Do not the philosophies of Sartre and Marx illustrate this primacy of artistic activity – in different ways, perhaps as two extremes (but, as opposites, within the same genus)?

Although the opposite – the exclusive primacy of moral activity – is rare today, it has occurred. Moral man then absorbs *homo faber*. (A certain degradation of Christian morality can engender such attitudes.) End overrides with such force that it rejects any question of efficiency. Friendship suffices! This is abnormal for human life, yet it is less horrible than the exaltation of efficiency, because respect for the other is not destroyed. The philosophy of Gabriel Marcel is an illustration of this tendency, his attempts as a playwright show it well.

Before considering the third experience, cooperation, let us note that these two human activities (artistic and moral), which develop in a certain becoming, each have their own immanent fruits which qualify and ennoble *homo faber* and *homo amicus* from within, allowing each of them to exercise his proper activity with greater nobility, facility, and rapidity. These immanent fruits are deeply rooted in our vital powers, i.e., our practical intellect, our will, and even our sensitive powers. These are what have been called the *habitus*[4] of art and virtue.

It is an undeniable fact: in forging we become a blacksmith; in dancing we become a dancer. In the very exercise of work, these dispositions and determinations are born in us and slowly grow. We thereby become a qualified laborer, a master blacksmith . . .

Here we must specify the different *habitus* of art, which can be born in us and, in a certain way, seal the major alliances of our practical intellect with our different external senses, through the imagination: the alliance of intellect and sight (pictorial art), intellect and hearing (musical art), intellect and touch (the art of sculpture and dance), intellect and taste (the art of viticulture), intellect and smell (the art of perfume).

There are also other *habitus* of art: the quite varied ones related to the skills of the artisan (crafts). These no longer stem immediately from the external senses, but from man's needs for fulfillment, development, and well-being.

Technique is characterized by the ever-increasing importance of tools and methods, for what is sought is no longer a well-made, beautiful and useful work but an economically profitable work. We pass from artisanal art to virtuosity.

Let us indeed distinguish the *habitus* and disposition of art from skill and virtuosity, which, precisely speaking, are only acquired qualities that allow for greater flexibility in execution. Skill and virtuosity have more to do with method and an instrument's efficiency than with inspiration and creative choice. Is it not this type of quality which characterizes a technician?

Parallel to the development of artistic activity is the acquisition of virtue involved in the development of moral activity, the acquisition of 'operative' *habitus* which enable the moral intention to develop and in

4 An acquired, stable disposition which ennobles the faculty that has acquired it, enabling it to act with greater perfection (for example, prudence qualifies the practical intellect, allowing it to order means to ends). [-Trans.]

the process grow, without being undermined by imaginary things through fear of the effort or fight required as soon as execution begins. Work has struggles of its own. Moral activity also has struggles, but these struggles are not the same; they are more internal.

We shall not reconsider here the complete genesis of the various virtues by seeing how they are acquired in our different moral activities exercised through what we call the 'concupiscible' and the 'irascible',[5] and how they always involve not only the will but a rectifying of our intentions with a view to the end being pursued. We shall only enumerate the various acquired moral virtues, according to their order of nobility.

The primary moral virtue is prudence. Prudence perfects our practical intellect by enabling it to be fixed in the intention of the desired end and consider everything that must be done (immediately or mediately) in the light of this intention. In this sense we can say that prudence rectifies practical reason, constituting it as 'right reason.' Prudence thus dispels what is imaginary, which always threatens to impede the deep intention that binds us to our end and prevent it from being limpid and conscious of its demands. Even more explicitly, prudence dispels what stems from the imagination and the passions which might lead us to choose the easier means, those most connatural to our passional affectivity. It gives us an interior acuteness which allows us opportunely to engage the act of the *imperium*, the act of command, despite the fear of failure and possible struggles.

The virtue of justice determines our voluntary appetite in its respect for another's rights. We must indeed struggle against our deeply rooted natural egoism which constantly turns us in on ourselves, hindering us from truly respecting the other's rights and, consequently, from loving him.

The virtue of fortitude ennobles our 'irascible,' that is, our passional appetite for sensible goods which are difficult to acquire. Fortitude keeps our passional appetite from getting uselessly carried away when faced with certain obstacles which seem to prevent us from acquiring these goods. In other words, it allows us not to get angry whenever we are faced with what appears to be a disorder. The virtue of fortitude ennobles our irascible and places it at the service of our practical intellect perfected by prudence. It allows us to use this passional élan to

5 The 'concupiscible' and the 'irascible,' as well as the will and the intellect, are studied in greater detail in the philosophy of the living being. For a definition of the 'concupiscible' and the 'irascible,' see below, pages 69–74.

conquer sensible goods which are difficult to attain. It allows us to be victorious over struggles by subjecting ourselves to 'right reason.'

While the virtue of fortitude rectifies the 'irascible,' the virtue of temperance ennobles the 'concupiscible' passions (those which are directed towards immediate sensible goods), preventing them from overwhelming us with their vehemence and extreme spontaneity. These always risk preceding us. The virtue of temperance, especially, resists what is imaginary because it tends to present immediate sensible goods to us as indispensable and necessary (as though we could not live without them). This virtue allows us to distance ourselves from the overly vehement attraction of an immediate sensible good. It helps us to relativize the good and order it to a superior, spiritual good. This is very obvious in friendship. There is always the risk of the passional aspect of a sensible presence gaining the upper hand. We risk no longer seeking the other out of love for him but for our own enjoyment, because his sensible presence attracts us, exciting our passions and even our sexual instinct (or drive). The vehemence of the sensible good – especially when it arouses our sexual instinct – risks stifling true personal, spiritual love. We thus see why the virtue of temperance, like fortitude, is necessary for keeping the love in friendship alive. Fortitude helps us not to disappoint our friend regarding the support he expects in difficult moments, in the struggles which, because of our love, become *our* struggles and require *our* cooperation and *our* effort.

We can also readily understand the necessity for the virtue of justice: respect for the rights of a friend are indispensable if the love in friendship is to continue to exist. A lack of respect for the rights of the other is capable of breaking friendship, because it shows that the friend does not love his friend for himself, but only for his own satisfaction.

These four virtues are called 'cardinal' because they are, as it were, the great axes of the other virtues. Indeed, the other moral virtues rest upon them. Because they are capable of preserving friendship, they allow it truly to blossom, and so deeply structure our moral personality.

It would be very interesting at this point to discern the different characteristics of moral freedom and artistic freedom. Very often we confuse these two types of freedom and attribute to moral freedom what is true only of artistic freedom. This is what Sartre did when he spoke of freedom.

The freedom of an artist is undoubtedly very fundamental, for an artist can want to realize – or refuse to realize – a specific work which is asked of him. He is free to say yes or no. Regarding the work that he is capable of realizing, he is his own master. Certainly he can be constrained to accept the work for other motives. If he needs money, for example, he can accept an offer which does not interest him as an artist (but that is another matter). To accept or not to accept because something conforms or does not conform to his artistic inspiration, his mentality as artist, his actual preoccupations, is the norm to which he refers in order to judge and give or withhold his assent. Thus, ultimately, his current artistic inspiration – and all that it implies – allows an artist to judge or discern what he can or cannot realize. Let us further specify that it is from what he estimates he can realize (the possible) that he chooses the matter and the tools for the realization of this possible. The more this possible is original and his own, the more an artist gains freedom with respect to all that is proposed to him. Now this possible, born of inspiration, in a certain way involves the negation of all that currently is. This is the *sine qua non* condition for the possible. Consequently, the 'annihilation' of everything the artist bears within himself, his interior world, his *vécu*,[6] is necessary for this possible to appear in its originality.

Such freedom, which is wholly relative to the inspiration of an artist, therefore has a subjective criterion. Only the artist can judge. He is his own master. He alone knows. He alone sees.

The freedom of a friend is completely different. Its exercise is based on love and takes shape in a choice. Does a friend not *freely* choose his friend as friend? He chooses him because he can allow him to love fully and be truly happy. And he chooses him because he loves him. If he rejects him, it is because he either no longer loves him or does not love him enough. It is love that enables him to make the free choice, and it is in reference to love that he does so. Love enables him to choose and urges him to choose freely. Love also enables him to reject and urges him to reject this choice freely. Love for a personal good, and the intention with respect to this good, considered as a pursued end, serve as an interior norm. They serve as the interior norm for judging whether the friend is this good and this end and, consequently, whether he is someone whom I freely choose or, on the contrary, someone who cannot be this good and this end.

Freedom of choice also appears with other choices that I make in the light of prudence, in order to attain an end which I do not yet possess. Before my friend has freely chosen me, for instance, I myself may desire

6 The subjective repercussions of experience upon an individual; experience to the extent that it is lived within.

him, and do my utmost to make him choose me. I shall then choose certain means to get closer to him. For example, I may become interested in those who are close to him. If I consider it more efficacious, I can freely choose one means over another. This freedom is based upon the good-end that one seeks, and it implies judging the relationship between the means, a relative good, and the end sought as an absolute good.

Thus these two types of freedom are completely different. Yet each of them involves the intellect, which judges the relationship between a particular means or a particular realization, and a particular end or a particular pursued ideal. Because this relation does not involve a necessary connection, our will remains free to choose one means over another. It can accept or refuse to engage itself.

To understand better the character of each of these freedoms, we can consider the problem of error and fault in man's practical activity. Both have their source in this activity, and both limit it, but in completely different ways. Fault is always voluntary and conscious. Error, however, can be either conscious or unconscious. When error is conscious, the artist willfully diminishes the result – the efficiency – of his artistic activity. When it is unconscious, the result clearly suffers but, above all, the error demonstrates the limits of the artist's work.

The error of which we speak here is located in the practical intellect. That is why it manifests – when it is unconscious – a flaw in that intellect. Contrary to what is held in the famous Platonic theory, according to which error is always due to ignorance, fault is always in the will and does not necessarily imply a flaw in the intellect. Thus ignorance cannot be the proper cause of either fault or error, yet it is very often an element of both.

Artistic activity can know certain errors, certain failures, which arise from circumstances outside the artist – the indetermination of the matter upon which he works, the faulty adaptation of the instruments employed, the milieu, those with whom he cooperates, etc. – or they can be expressly willed by the artist.

In moral activity, on the other hand, man can freely turn away from the spiritual good he considers an end, and from the means ordered to this end, in order to choose more immediate goods either closer to his sensitivity or more likely to exalt him. Here we see the philosophical problem of fault, voluntary moral activity which is no longer under the attraction of a personal good loved as an end, but drawn to and swept away by a more immediately attained sensible good and by exalted love of self. This is our first discovery of the exaltation of the subject. Man no longer seeks that which perfects him, his end, a real good that transcends him, but the exaltation of his ego — which involves the exaltation of his own judgment and intuition.

With willful artistic error, it is not specifically the operating subject — man — but the idea, the possible, that which can be accomplished, which is exalted. The artist's inspiration is exalted, and not the person who operates, the subject. With practical error in artistic activity, the ideal form is exalted and overwhelms man. With a fault of pride, man voluntarily exalts himself in his autonomy, his own judgment, of which he becomes the immediate measure.

5

THE PHILOSOPHY OF COMMUNITY

The third experience in the practical order is that of cooperation with a view to a common realization, that is, something made together that is to be part of the common good. It is the experience of a practical commitment in which we are no longer the only one concerned, in which we depend upon the will of another or others. This experience is therefore more complex than the preceding two; it involves elements of *making*, and of *acting* (doing).

Indeed, we are no longer dealing here with the experience of friendship. The experience of friendship certainly implies that friends together realize a common work, but this is the immediate consequence of their love, a 'common fruit' which renders their love concrete. Strictly speaking, it is not a new experience. And yet the person with whom we cooperate must have some trust in us, and we ourselves must have some trust in him; otherwise, there will not be cooperation but only juxtaposition and, as a result, a rivalry which rapidly introduces conflict between those who are supposed to work together. The mutual trust required in cooperation implies a reciprocal personal love, with a desire to respect fully the personality of each in its originality and otherness. This mutual trust allows a reciprocal commitment: we commit ourselves to realizing a specific work together. This commitment implies a certain mutual responsibility; aware of our own capacities and limits, and those of the other person, we want to help and serve one another.

The experience of cooperation cannot be reduced to the experience each one has of his own work, for there is no efficient cooperation if we are not attentive to the other person's work. Cooperation, of course, implies some efficiency. We are realizing a common work together. It does not matter if it is a utilitarian or an artistic work. It is, in any case, a commitment engaging our artistic activity, our *facere*.

Moreover, the experience of cooperation, in human community, implies that there are at least three persons involved. Friendship occurs between two persons who have chosen one another and who are one another's end. Cooperation at the community level requires a minimum of three persons, for at least two commit themselves to doing a common

work for the benefit of another. It is this common work that determines
the mutual commitment of the two and is received by a third (here we
see the difference between a common work and a friend who is chosen
by his friend for himself[1]). Justice immediately appears, for the work is
completed by at least two persons, and this work can be received and
used by a third.

This work is truly a 'common good' in the sense that it is the good of
the three persons and therefore plays the role of *end* for each of them, an
end that truly finalizes. This common good is a result, a work. It is the
common work of at least two people, and so cannot be reduced to a
single source. The more numerous those who contribute to the
completion of a common work, the fruit of their labor, the more
the work surpasses the fruit of each one's labor taken individually, and
the more it can be considered a common good capable of being an end
for various human activities. That is why a common good is both what
each individual has realized and what finalizes each individual, permit-
ting a better life. Such is the complexity of a common good.

In cooperation, no matter how simple it is, there is always at least
one who orders and one who obeys. That is why cooperation at the
community level takes on various forms: that of the person who orders,
that of the person who obeys, that of the person who uses the common
fruit. In order to understand the character of cooperation, it is good to
have experienced these different forms, so that we can grasp what they
have in common and what is proper to each of them.

Are we not faced here with the essential first division of work? To do
away with it in the name of idealized egalitarianism leads to the
suppression of all cooperation. It leads to everyone working for himself
and considering only himself. This, however, is the suppression of
community. Only an aggregate of individuals remains, every man for
himself, with no common goal.

For Aristotle, this first division of labor is natural in the sense that it
is analogous to the distinction between the body and the soul. Our
spiritual soul commands and orders, our body obeys and executes, and
both are engaged in all our human activities in the practical order. In
human cooperation there is always someone more clear-sighted, more
experienced, more capable from the standpoint of knowledge, and
another who is more physically vigorous and capable of execution. The
former is more intellectually developed and the latter more disposed to
immediate efficiency. It is to their mutual benefit to unite (while
respecting each other's qualities) and to cooperate (each according to his

1 Literally 'in his proper person.'

own ability) in realizing a common work, a work that could never be done if each went his own way, competing with the other. All this should be obvious as everyday experience.

This cooperation, however, can only last and grow if it is truly for the common good of those who comprise the community, and if the various members of the community are conscious of it and recognize it. As soon as a community is no longer profitable to all its members, it only profits some and the others are wronged. In such a case, cooperation cannot last without the need for heroism, for basic justice is no longer respected. All the members work, sacrifice, and give of their strength and time, so normally all should benefit, or at least have a real hope of benefitting. It can happen that one person temporarily benefits more than another, but then some sort of compensation is necessary, an assurance that this will change to benefit those who have toiled.

If cooperation is for the common good of all the members of a community, then the qualities of all should usually be developed as much as possible. It is then easier for everyone to recognize the qualities of their collaborators, even to the extent of being happy about cooperating with them, truly benefitting from their gifts and striving for mutual complementarity. Is not this the perfect *concordia* that we desire for every truly human community, which can be realized, at least temporarily, if the number of participants remains limited? Notice here that *number* is a constitutive element. Quantity only conditioned activity in the previous experiences; here it gives it a new dimension.

But if there is a 'spectator' with an agenda or ideology, who looks at human cooperation with the intention of destroying it, it will be easy for him to see the weak points, the shortcomings, of the persons involved, and to label these persons for all to know, which will discourage them and lead them to revolt. A spectator from outside cannot judge the true inter-subjectivity involved in voluntary cooperation. In this sense, can we not say that cooperation ought to reject anyone who wants only to be a spectator? A spectator remains on the outside and cannot truly make a practical judgment. Cooperation is always undermined, destroyed, or sabotaged in this way, to the detriment of all.

If the common good is the fruit of cooperation, then there are various forms of common good. This enables us to distinguish different human communities, each specified by one of these common goods.

The first – the most basic and most natural common good – is that of the family. The family involves friendship between a man and a woman, between husband and wife. It is founded on their reciprocal free choice. Capable of fruitfulness, this love is the procreator of a third member: a child. At this point there is community in the strong sense. A child is the fruit of the reciprocal love between spouses, but he is also a person who is *other* than his parents, with his own rights. The family community must respect these rights, especially because they are those of a small infant who is not conscious of them and cannot defend himself; he is helpless. His parents must therefore take care of him and raise him, and this can only be done in love. This community can only exist in and through love, in and through the friendship between spouses, and their paternal and maternal love for the child who must be welcomed and carried. This community is above and beyond justice.

The common good of the family allows the child to become an autonomous human person, with a capacity to discover his own end and orient himself, in a free choice, towards this end. For this, a family milieu must be created, with a certain material and spiritual well-being, which permits and favors this blossoming.

If the family milieu depends primarily upon the love of the parents for one another, any rift in this love leads immediately to a family that no longer has the desired human warmth. The family milieu also depends upon the efficiency of the parents' work and upon the cultural milieu in which the family develops.

The family is present as a fundamental community but, far from excluding other communities, it calls for them. These others are work communities and the political community.

Work communities, which have become so important in our time that they often seek to usurp absolute rights, have a very precise common good: increasingly efficient production for the benefit of all their members. Production has undergone particularly rapid growth with the development of technology. It is clear that the common good of a community of artisans is entirely different from the common good of a modern factory. We are no longer faced with only two complementary modes in cooperative work: the work of someone who commands and the work of someone who obeys. A third factor has intervened: that of the machine, a perfected tool which requires considerable investment because of its perfection. This perfected tool, which is only a tool and should only condition work, often transforms it very radically. Indeed, the machine often no longer belongs to those who work, but to an anonymous power that imposes its own demands. The machine cost 'this much,' and so must bring in 'this much' for those who bought it. Thus the price of works realized by the labor of workers and those on whom they depend, who command them, cannot depend solely upon these two. It must take into account the investment in machines. This is where what we call 'capital' comes into play. The question of cooperation then becomes more complex, for the various elements must be taken into account and ordered according to their value. Here, ideologies easily intervene and distort the problem by idealizing it. To consider the intervention of an investment in a machine, that is, its worth, as necessarily being an alienating power to which we must be opposed in the name of workers' rights, leads to considering class struggle as a basic principle shedding light on the search for justice. If the machine belongs to the 'capitalist bourgeoisie,' it exploits the work of the 'proletariat' and alienates it. Do not the 'capitalist bourgeoisie,' via machines, purchase the labor of workers? This injustice must then be crushed by opposing it as much as possible. To be efficient, this opposition must come from the power of trade unions which claim to seek the good of the worker, but unfortunately these are often executive organs of certain political ideologies.

It is clear that in our industrialized world there is much injustice. It is clear that those who have financial power easily consider themselves to have all the rights. But in order to fight injustice, we must not let ourselves be guided by ideologies whose positions are diametrically opposed; they can also consider only profit, without taking man's good into account. The only way to fight injustice is to discover a truly human economy. *Man* is the one who works. *Man* is the one who invests his wealth. The different means and various powers must be at the service of man's good, his blossoming, and they must not lose sight of this end. Money has value only in relation to man. It is a powerful means, but it does not confer authority. Authority belongs only to someone who thinks, organizes, and orders the various means with a view to man's good.

We must recognize, however, that it is difficult to take a step back. When we are in the midst of struggle, we are always tempted to use the adversary's weapons and adopt his method. This is a poor tactic, however, for the adversary's method was developed with a different goal in mind, a purpose for which it is adapted. It will necessarily be less efficient if we want it to serve another purpose for which it is less adapted; so we are beaten beforehand. We must therefore have the courage and intelligence to take up the problem at its root, in what it is essentially. We do this by determining the essential elements in truly human cooperation, cooperation for everyone's good, cooperation that respects everyone's rights, and appreciates those rights in a healthy vision of man. It is obvious that money is at the service of the working man, and not the working man at the service of money. The working man must understand that, in today's historical context, various elements intervene, and that it is better to cooperate with them than to try to crush them. Money is not bad in itself. It all depends on how it is used. It is its usage that is good or bad. It is thus the evil, abusive use of money that we fight and not those who possess it. Here we see the importance of focusing upon *man*, a perspective that ideologies, whether right-wing or left-wing, have lost.

Beyond the community of workers there is the political community. It is important to recall the distinction between them because man cannot be reduced to being simply a worker. He has family roots that are natural to him and, in order to progress and discover all of the treasures of man, he needs a milieu of artistic culture and scientific and technological research. The common good of the political community is man's 'good living' (*bene vivere*), concord between citizens, and it consists in allowing the deepest blossoming of all that is human in man. A person who governs must therefore have a certain vision of man – for what is he made? what is his true happiness? – otherwise he cannot truly govern, that is, help to attain happiness. He can only seek to balance opposing forces at the economic, as well as ideological, level. Someone who wants truly to govern must use the power he holds to arouse in those who are subject to him a desire for unity and human trust in order to cooperate and avoid divisions, discords, and sterile ideological confrontations.

The political community must respect the familial community, because the latter has a more immediate natural foundation which allows the political community to survive. The political community must also respect the community of workers, but in a very different way, for the latter does not touch man directly in his nature, his life, or his first education, but in his need to blossom and his need for efficiency.

We must never forget that man's happiness is personal and that it cannot come from the common good. The latter must dispose to happiness, but it cannot directly bring happiness; it cannot be its immediate source. Each person must discover it for himself, either through the awakening of friendship or through adoration and contemplation of the First Being, who is either discovered through metaphysical knowledge or acknowledged by religious traditions.

Just as political authority must respect man's happiness (something that it cannot bring him), it must also respect the demands of friendship between spouses, and thus the fruitfulness of their love, procreation. It can give advice in this field, but it cannot intervene with a power of coercion.

It might be thought that a philosophy which seeks man's happiness has completed its analysis when it has considered these three parts of practical philosophy: the philosophy of work, the philosophy of friendship, and the philosophy of community. Yet it must develop in three new directions. It is really the search for man's happiness that keeps it from stopping at these three practical philosophies, because it has not yet discovered if he whom religious traditions refer to as the Creator, really exists. This is important; for if he is only a myth that helps man to behave himself and be just and good, then philosophy must acknowledge that man's happiness resides uniquely in friendship. But if God truly exists, and if our intellect can attain to him and contemplate him, then man's ultimate happiness is in adoring him and contemplating him. Religious myth awaits a deeper, purer knowledge, one that the philosopher can have at the end of his inquiry.

We must try to understand the necessity of that intellectual knowledge which is called 'speculative,' that is, ordered to the discovery of truth, unlike practical knowledge, which is ordered either to the realization of a work or to the rectitude of moral action. We must take up Marx's challenge: until now, philosophers have only interpreted the world; henceforth, we must transform it, transform man and the world. Really, there is no opposition between knowing the world and transforming the world, for it must be known to be transformed, and it must be transformed to be known more perfectly.

6

THE PHILOSOPHY OF NATURE

If we are attentive to the experience of work, we notice that it presupposes another experience. It presupposes a knowledge of matter. Work transforms matter and thereby gives us a certain knowledge of its capacity to be transformed. We could almost say that what we know then is matter as potential energy; but this presupposes that matter in itself (what it is) is known. There is indeed a certain knowledge of matter prior to its transformation, for we can touch it, smell it, and see it. This is obvious with an artisan. The joiner considers his wood before working it, and he chooses a particular type of wood with a view to the work to be realized. Thus there is an experience of matter prior to work.

Moreover, when we philosophically analyzed artistic activity, we specified that inspiration is, as it were, 'exemplary cause.' But does inspiration not presuppose a certain sensitive knowledge of the different qualities of the material realities in our universe? Inspiration is the principle for the realization of an artistic work, but it is not primary in an absolute sense. We always begin by knowing our universe and discovering its qualities, its light, before we have an interior illumination, an inspiration that allows us to say and express what we feel.

This immediate knowledge of the sensible, physical realities that surround us can be ordered towards work. It can also be a direct contact with the sensible qualities considered in themselves, in their proper splendor. Then what we have is a certain artistic experience. The painter looks at soil differently than the farmer who wants to plow it. It is certainly the same soil, but different aspects are considered.

We can also consider these sensible, physical realities for themselves, in so far as they exist as physical realities. This perspective is a certain experience stemming from the alliance of our intellect with the external senses, an experience that implies a judgment of existence. I then consider the soil on which I walk, which I touch, and seek to know it; and I affirm that it exists as a sensible, physical reality distinct from me, one which existed before me, and will most likely exist after me. The soil has different aspects. It is part of the universe in which I exist. Such an experience awakens admiration when I realize that I am now discovering a physical reality in its originality. Doubtless I have seen it before, perhaps many times, but I was only looking at it in a utilitarian fashion, to use it. I was not looking at it for itself, as an original reality with its own individuality. I now discover that it exists as a reality capable of being modified, transformed, and moved, but which, all the same, really exists, with its own existence, distinct from what I am. This reality, in its originality, is distinct from works of art, man-made realities, for it is something fundamental and primary, something in itself, prior to all the transformations that man can bring about.

With admiration, we question: What is this physical reality in its own fundamental character? This reality, distinct from a work of art, is determined and susceptible to being transformed both by the other realities that surround it – the milieu (the phenomenon of erosion, the slow disintegration of everything we see and touch) – and by man's work, whereby it assumes a new form, an expressive form or capacity for utilization, but thenceforth ceases to be a properly physical reality. This reality involves, therefore, matter capable of being modified, capable of receiving a new 'figure,' a new 'face.' It has something indivisible (certain qualities that we grasp by means of our external senses: the 'proper sensibles') and something divisible (the capacity for modification, for transformation). And yet physical realities have a certain unity in their existence, a unity which is especially manifest when we grasp what is fundamental in them, beyond the initially manifest complexity. In questioning and considering the fundamental unity in diversity (the proper qualities and their divisible substratum), our intellect discovers in each of these realities an immanent fundamental principle. This principle gives them their proper determination, their character, and their capacity for transformation. This radical principle is what the ancient Greeks called *physis*, nature.[1] Under ordinary conditions, we cannot say that 'all is in all,' for there are certain determinations which impose themselves: water is not earth, and earth is not air – although by making them undergo certain transformations (notably, with fire), we can change water into vapor and vapor can release energy similar to that in the solid realities called earth. This immanent principle which we call 'nature' possesses its own complexity. Nature possesses a proper determination called form-nature. It also possesses a proper indetermination called matter-nature. This explains both how a physical reality has certain unique qualities (it is such-and-such a reality: water, for example),

---

1 Let us not forget that *physis* comes from πηΨομαι (pephomai), to grow, and 'nature' from *nascio*, to be born. Hence the notions of movement and dynamism are always linked to those of nature.

and how it can, under the influence of the milieu or of a particular agent, undergo such profound transformation that it seems to become another reality. Matter-nature is so radical an indetermination that we cannot set a limit to it. This is being shown more and more. In the realities that we experience there are almost infinite capacities for transformation. Think, for example, about the disintegration of the atom. It is true that these are no longer natural but artificial transformations. Yet they use natural realities as 'matter' to be transformed. The day we end with something that can no longer be transformed by something else into something else, will be the day we reach a limit in the order of transformation; but we can never know if such a limit is transient or if we have touched something irreversible, a formal fixation, as it were, of all the 'evacuated' potentialities of matter. But is this possible in our universe? It is certainly not possible in the order of natural transformations; but is it not possible in the order of artificial transformations? Can we not artificially separate a particular form from a particular matter? Such separations always seem to go further, as the instruments are perfected, and limits cannot be set to such research. We then arrive at an artificial body which, in fact, can no longer be modified by something else and then escapes the conditions of our 'sublunar' world (the world of decomposition, or disintegration), as the ancients used to say.

This gives rise to an important question regarding end. Do the physical realities we experience have a proper end? And parallel to the question of an end is that of chance; if a physical reality is not moved towards its own end, it is moved by chance. Now, what is moved by chance does not have a proper cause; it therefore occurs accidentally.

It is obvious, however, that all natural realities are determined – even if they are capable of being transformed – and imply a certain order in their natural movement. They are not moved haphazardly; their natural movement possesses a certain orientation. There can, of course, be monstrosities and failures that arise from matter-nature and its radical indetermination, but because of form-nature we can say that natural movements are ordered and therefore imply a certain end. It is obviously not an end extrinsic to these realities, but an immanent end, an end engraved in the natural order of their movements. This form-nature, this end, is especially grasped in living beings and man, but it exists in the entire physical universe.

This allows us to specify natural movement: it is 'the act of that which is in potency (or 'potentiality') inasmuch as it is in potency,' as Aristotle says in his *Physics*. And this is still accurate, notwithstanding Bergson's criticism which, incidentally, does not attain to Aristotle's true thought. Natural movement is indeed what brings physical reality to completion, what actuates it. A physical body – which is a mobile body – is only in act when it is moved. A physical body, however, is never perfectly actuated; it always remains in potency, capable of being actuated. That is why, as a physical body, it cannot be at rest. The movement of physical realities is possessed by these realities. It is a flux, which is not a possession and is always in succession; as soon as it is, in the present moment, in the next moment, it no longer is. In and through the becoming of a physical reality we grasp the fragility of its being: 'the act of that which is in potency inasmuch as it is in potency.' The act emerges, yet it remains conditioned, limited by the potency from which it emerges. Potency is first and last in a physical reality. Consequently, physical reality only exists in its becoming. Although its act can be intellectually distinguished from its potency and its form from its matter, its act can never be existentially separated from its potency, nor its form from its matter, for the becoming of a physical reality is its being, and its becoming implies act and potency, form and matter.

Thereby we understand what characterizes the physical world: it never ceases to change. Although the saying attributed to Heraclitus is true – 'All things are in a state of flux,' – it only refers to one aspect of reality, for in this flux, this change, there is a certain intelligibility, a certain *logos* which Heraclitus himself grasped, although he was unable to express it clearly. There is a form, a determination, a *physis* as Aristotle would say, in every moved physical reality.

The great difficulty we have in understanding *physis*, nature, arises from the fact that we have difficulty in acquiring a philosophical perspective of contemplative knowledge. This is because of modern scientific culture, or the influence of Hegelian and materialistic dialectic, or the ascendancy of phenomenology – all of which stop this discovery and hinder this philosophical induction. This qualitative induction – to differentiate it from a Baconian induction – can only be done from a judgment of existence of the qualities of moved physical realities and of the order of these qualities which, within becoming itself, requires a going beyond, i.e., the discovery of a principle, a cause, a source of these qualities, a source of this becoming. Modern scientific knowledge, although it does not reject the judgment of existence nor the existence of these proper qualities, only looks at what is capable of being measured. The quantitative aspect is highlighted and becomes foremost. That is why nature, principle and cause, can no longer be discovered. We only grasp laws, relationships of constancy and regularity between anteriority and posteriority, necessary connections in the behavior of physical realities. As for Hegelian dialectic, it only grasps the formalization of becoming. It does not grasp physical reality, nor its act, nor its fundamental potency. It only grasps the opposition between contraries – formalized as an opposition between contradictories – because the contraries are considered in their own right, as it were, beyond their subjects. We discover the synthesis of these contradictories, that is, their formalization made explicit. It is not nature – the radical principle of that-which-is-moved – which is grasped, but the formalization of contraries involved in movement.

As for phenomenological method, it grasps only the intelligibility of reality. We start with an idea and remain in the idea; we only grasp our idea, even if we claim to attain to reality. In a phenomenological perspective, we only attain to the intelligibility of that-which-is-moved, the intelligibility of the physical reality, its form and not its potentiality. Thus nature, as immanent principle of that-which-is-moved, is not attained. Mobile being, as mobile being, is not grasped.

Without lingering here on the diversity of physical movements, let us just point out that becoming is manifold; it possesses a certain diversity. There is movement according to quality (movement of alteration), movement according to quantity (movement of growth), movement according to place (local movement), and movement of generation which reaches that which is most radical in a physical being (this movement is especially manifest in the reproduction of living things). Physical being is mobile in its various dimensions, its various qualities, all that it is.

Two other extremely important questions are linked to that of the movement of the nature of a physical body: *time* and *place*. These are important questions for human life. Since Kant, these have been regarded as two 'categories' – time and space – which express what is fundamental in our psychical behavior. It is by time and place that we fundamentally situate ourselves in relation to the universe and its historical development.

What is time? What is place? Is there a void in our universe? These are questions that philosophers have always asked, precisely because they stem from something very fundamental in our psychical behavior.

Time and place can only be grasped in relation to physical realities in so far as these are moved. Time is understood from the succession of that-which-is-moved. The intellect orders the succession and gives it unity by measuring it. This is how time appears. Is time not the 'measure of movement,' that which gathers the succession of movement, and gives it a certain unity? Time implies the past, the present moment, and the future; yet only the present moment *is*, for the past is no longer and the future is not yet. Only the present moment is the measure of that-which-is-moved, while the future and the past are measures of the succession of movement, which, again, only exists in relation to that-which-is-moved. This manifests the fragility of that-which-is-moved, of physical reality. Physical reality only exists in the present moment. But our intellect can speak of the past and the future, for it is beyond becoming and has the capacity to measure it. Thus time, as measure of movement, only exists in our human intellect. But it has a foundation in the existence of 'that-which-is-moved', thanks to the present moment, its measure.

It is perhaps time which best helps us to understand philosophical idealism in which the human intellect measures the physical world, the whole of reality, the whole of being, and gives it its meaning. Reality has no meaning for an idealist when it is not known; it does not really exist. This is understandable when we realize that experience, bound to the judgment of existence, primarily regards that-which-is-moved. Now, that-which-is-moved is bound to time, measured by the present moment. Consequently, our intellectual life, the development of our intellect, is conditioned by time. It is easy to conclude, therefore – as some have done – that our intellectual life is *determined* by time and, by this very fact, that how we know time determines how we know being, how we know that-which-is. Is this not the deepest confusion of our intellect – confusing that which determines the judgment of existence and that which conditions it? 'That-which-is' determines the judgment of existence. How that-which-is exists, conditions the judgment of existence. That which exists in our physical world exists as moved. It exists in becoming, and becoming is measured by time. Thus time formalizes the conditioning of that-which-is.

As that-which-is-moved is measured by the present moment, 'that-which-is-moved' finds its end in *place*. Is it not place in which 'that-which-is-moved' naturally rests? If there is an order in our physical universe, the more perfect body is the end of the less perfect one; the more perfect is the end of the less perfect by drawing or attracting it, which it can only do in direct contact with it. This is how the more perfect body is the place of the less perfect body – that is, if the less perfect body is in direct contact with the more perfect body. Notice the quite particular and imperfect character of this end which, in comparison to the end of the spirit (man's happiness), is but a distant shadow.[2]

---

2 We could establish the following analogy: the immediately superior body is to the inferior body what a friend is to his friend. Is not a friend the 'place' of his friend? The only difference is that the inferior body has not chosen the superior body.

In an idealistic perspective, place has become the category of space. We can understand how. If, in setting aside its proper end, the ordered dynamism of moved reality is no longer considered, then only its becoming is considered; and this becoming is considered as doubly conditioned by time and space, for it must necessarily be placed in relation to the entire universe. In this perspective, time and space become the 'categories' that render physical realities intelligible.

A realistic philosopher cannot renounce the analysis of the physical world. Why? Because his body, capable of being moved and trans-formed, makes him a part of the universe. Man is 'part' of the universe by his body. He is localized and measured by time. He is capable of undergoing the influence of this whole that is the universe. He is conditioned by it and cannot abstract himself from it. That is why a philosopher cannot, with respect to the universe, be content with the knowledge of the physical and astronomical sciences, interesting as they may be. He must maintain a realistic philosophical perspective on matter, nature and movement, time and place, and clearly show what distinguishes his perspective from that of the physical sciences. Indeed, for a philosopher and for a scientist, the meaning of matter is completely different.

7

THE PHILOSOPHY OF THE LIVING BEING

As the experience of work required a new understanding of matter prior to work, so the experience of friendship requires a new understanding of the living being, an understanding more radical than that of friendship. A friend is a friend because he is first a living being.

It is the question of death – the fundamental 'break' or 'fissure' in a living being – which, because it imposes itself upon us, obliges us (according to the genetic order) to go beyond the affective knowledge that unites friends. It is true that we do not have a direct experience of death, which is why it always remains for us something unknown that frightens us and fills us with anxiety. We cannot overcome it; it is beyond us. Moreover, death is a limit for philosophical knowledge. It shows man his limits. It stands like a wall before him, a wall which he cannot clear. What lies behind it? Even if a philosopher can progressively understand that there is something in man distinct from his body, something that accounts for his capacity for interiority, 'something' that cannot possibly disappear with death, he cannot know how this 'something' might remain, how it might exist or live after death. It truly remains an enigma for him.

The philosopher does not have a direct experience of death, but he can have an indirect experience of it when, for example, he witnesses the death of a friend, a loved one. At that moment, death causes a terrible void, an irreparable absence. Someone who was there, who was so present even in his weakness and his agony, is suddenly no longer there. He no longer listens. He no longer sees. He no longer responds. There are no more gestures. There is no more breathing. His friend is no longer present.

With death a radical break occurs and, before this break, man feels his helplessness; he cannot undo it. The break is too profound and too absolute. It is, as it were, an abyss that separates two friends. One remains here, alone, and the whereabouts of the other is unknown. Religious traditions speak of Hades, of the kingdom of shadows, to veil humanity's ignorance and manifest its hope, but our intellect can know nothing of what happens to a friend after his death. It can only assert the negation of his former life, a rupture with respect to a former state of life. Our heart, the heart of a friend, can only suffer painfully when it recognizes that death implies the total absence of the one we love. Our human sensitivity can only be silent before the cold silence of death. We are shattered when faced with the death of a friend, for we carry his death within; and if we allow ourselves to be completely taken with our feelings, there is nothing left to do but disappear with our friend. Does not death call for death?

The death of a friend shows that the love which united us to him was not substantial; otherwise our friend would not have died. Our love would have prevented his death. Despite and against our love for him, he is dead. Do we not touch here the limit of our love, its radical powerlessness? We thereby discover the profound distinction between friend and living being, between love and life. No matter how strong it may be, and although it aspires to never ending, love cannot be victorious over death. It must yield in spite of itself. This therefore leads to the question, 'What is a living being?' In order to respond, we need to reflect upon our experience of living beings.

Although we do not have an experience of death, we can have an experience of a living being (that we are). We experience that we breathe, eat, see, walk, think, and love ... All these activities are characteristic operations of the living beings that we are. They depend upon us. We are their proper source. We truly move ourselves in these various operations; we are not simply moved. Because of this, the living being that we experience in a privileged way is ourselves. We can only experience in a privileged way, as vital operations, our own operations (walking, eating, feeling, thinking, loving, etc.). We grasp them as vital operations which depend intimately upon us, vital operations of which we are the immediate origin; they come from us. We cannot experience someone else's operations in the same way, similar and close as he may be to us, for we only experience them from the outside – as we experience physical realities (those which are moved) from the outside. We experience our own vital operations, however, as coming from us; we experience them from the inside.

It is not, strictly speaking, in a reflective approach that we grasp them, although we do have a certain self-lucidity which allows us to grasp them in their originality, i.e., as vital operations proceeding from a living being that lives, that moves itself. We can understand how some have spoken of the intuition of a 'vital *élan*' to express what is unique in this intimate experience. Yet the danger of such an expression is readily understood. It emphasizes the duration of the vital operation as such, rather than the special manner in which the vital operation exists. It seems preferable to insist upon the original character of our experience of walking, thinking, etc. For it is a particular, concretely existing, vital operation that we experience, and not the characteristic common to all vital operations. We do not experience a vital *élan* per se but this or that vital operation.

The proper character and diversity of these operations can arouse astonishment in us. Our physical body, inasmuch as it is alive, is part of the universe, yet it possesses an autonomy which is manifested in these various operations, because they have their source *in* the living being. These operations originate in the living body, and are ordered to it; they are for the proper flourishing of the living being. A living being has its own rhythm of life, yet all the while depends upon its milieu. It uses the milieu; it assimilates certain elements of it and thereby creates for itself a whole milieu for life, growth, irradiation – we might even say, for 'glory.' This is manifest with certain large living beings: an oak or a cedar creates for itself a milieu in the forest in which to live. A lion or an elephant similarly creates one in its own environment. If he is fully alive, man also creates a certain milieu for himself and his family: his hut, his garden, his hunting ground. Through the milieu it creates, a living being dominates its own little plot of land, and the more fully alive it is, the more it leaves its mark and the more it attracts everything toward itself. This emergence of a living being from the physical world, which it transforms by appropriating and assimilating, is something remarkable and astonishing. Hence the question, 'What is a living being?' 'What grants it such domination?'

From the perspective of this question, we must return to the experience of our vital operations to try to discover that by which they are what they are in themselves (what makes them what they are), and why they exist. In other words, we must discover their principles and their proper causes.

In the light of this question, we must also ask what might be true in religious traditions which speak of the soul and body of the living being *par excellence* which is man, and what might be true when they speak of the immortality of this soul, of life after death. Ought they to be considered myths which imply a duality (soul–body) that is unacceptable today? Indeed, many of our contemporaries, because of their philosophical position – whether positivistic, materialistic, or phenomenological – reject the distinction between the soul and the body and consider it completely outdated. What is interesting to note is that the method of biological science only grasps the conditioning of a living being, its various ways of reacting. Its methodology only attains to what is measurable in a living being: its behavior and the effects of its vital operations. Biology cannot immediately grasp what qualitatively characterizes a vital operation in so far as it moves itself. A biologist's scientific method can say nothing of the soul; if the soul exists he cannot attain to it. Thus, if a biologist, by virtue of a positivistic attitude, considers his scientific knowledge to be the only objective knowledge, he will conclude that the soul does not exist, for his scientific method cannot detect it. But he forgets that scientific knowledge is but one particular type of human knowledge. He forgets that the objectivity of human knowledge is not only the objectivity of scientific knowledge. The judgment of existence attests to it.

The same thing can be said of a dialectical materialist who, a priori, only considers as real what is material, what is observable by scientific method.

Nor can phenomenological philosophy speak of the soul about which religious traditions speak, for it remains at a descriptive level, at the level of our immediate consciousness, and of what is grasped in and through a reflective approach. Now, it is precisely our consciousness of our vital operations which leads us to discover a deep unity, that of the 'self,' which is a constant throughout our vital activities. Certainly these activities appear complex, yet none of them are grasped as separate from our body. That is why phenomenology necessarily affirms that, while our living being is complex, it is also 'one,' and that it can only be complex in its oneness. We cannot speak of the distinction between the soul and the body, therefore, for this distinction does not correspond to the consciousness we have of our vital operations in their complexity and their unity.

Here is a point about which we must be very lucid (and where phenomenology helps): we cannot be conscious of the distinction between soul and body, nor can we grasp it in a reflective method. The phenomenological method, however, is not the only philosophical method. We must, therefore, continue our investigation.

Note, first, that if we reflect upon our vital operations, we are obliged to recognize that, thanks to these operations and in and through them, there is a very intimate phenomenon of interiority which others, who view us from without, cannot grasp. We must then ask: What are the vital operations which imply this interiority? Although everything viewed from the exterior can be explained by the living, organic body, the interiority of our vital operations cannot. What is the interiority that we carry within ourselves, which manifests itself to our consciousness through our vital operations? Some speak of the 'psyche,' the complex and subtle realm of which we are more or less conscious, and which even implies the subconscious.[1] This realm exists, in a manner other than our biological life – but it is real. Indeed, our psyche can be a source of disturbance in our biological life. What is this psychical realm within us? From where does it come? Is there not an intimate love of self, of our own person – of which we can become conscious – which is at the root of interiority and of the psychical realm? This love cannot be reduced to love for the body. We can discern (if we have a certain interior life) between a sensitive love for our body, its beauty, its harmony, its flexibility, its power, and a deeper love for ourselves. Thereby we can have a certain affective knowledge of 'something' in us, in our inmost selves, beyond the visible and even beyond all psychical change. This 'something' is more present to us than everything else. It is what is most precious in us. It is the source of everything else. Is this not precisely what religious traditions call 'soul,' the spiritual soul, or the spirit; that is, the hidden, intimate source of our human life and our radical interiority? We do not know what this 'soul' is; but we can affirm that there is 'something' which seems distinct from our body, which is more present to us than our own body, 'something' which is intimately present and is the source of an intimate sense of self.

Such an understanding is insufficient for the philosopher, for it is too affective and incommunicable. It remains a certain interior experience, doubtless very deep, but also very obscure and inexpressible. It is the affective feeling of a presence, a hidden source upon which all our vital operations depend.

The better to discover this hidden source called 'soul,' we must return to our various vital operations – those of respiration, nutrition, sensation, the passions, walking, running, thought, the will, etc. – and examine them and seek the 'why' of their diversity and their deep unity.

These operations all come from us and take root in us; and each manifests a particular aspect of the living being that we are: we breathe, eat, feel, suffer, walk, think, love. All these vital operations appear to have the same radical source. It is always the same living being that moves itself in different ways. All these operations have the same final end: the development of the living being, its perfection and blossoming. Although we can distinguish various vital operations, we cannot separate them, for they have a unity more fundamental than their diversity. Thus these operations necessarily have a unique and radical source beyond the diversity. This hidden source is indeed what we call

1 We will later specify the philosophical meaning we give this word.

'soul.' The radical source of unity remains immanent to the body and informs it, for we are 'one' in our vital operations and our life, and the body itself is engaged in these vital operations – in different ways, but always engaged and present. My body is obviously engaged in a very special way in breathing, nutrition, and sensation, but it is also engaged when I think, for 'I' cannot be abstracted from my body. There is a unique source of life in us. In informing an organic body, this source has a certain complexity which expresses itself in a variety of vital operations.

Let us be more precise and say that this hidden source called soul is truly a principle, a cause of life for the organic body that it informs and animates. It is discovered as that which brings about the unity within our vital operations. It is indeed an indivisible principle and cause of (our) life. In this sense there is a substantial unity between soul and body. Their real distinction, which is the fruit of analysis, does not imply an existential separation, but a deep unity of being and life. Man, composed of a spiritual soul and a body, is a living being who is substantially 'one.' This is not a mere union, a reciprocal relation between two things which unite and cooperate – as Plato thought. For Plato, the unity of soul and body is an accidental union. The body is the 'tomb' of the soul,[2] and it is only by separating, and consequently freeing itself, from the body that the soul can live its own life: a contemplative life. In a Platonic perspective – partially adopted by Descartes – the body burdens the soul in its contemplative spiritual *élan*.

This philosophical perspective is correct in so far as the body manifests our limits. It conditions our vital activities, and often arrests our most intimate and spiritual *élans*; and it causes fatigue in work. This does not mean, however, that the body is united to the soul in an accidental way. As previously pointed out, all our vital operations – varied as they may be – imply a radical unity of being and life: *I* breathe, *I* eat, *I* think. The body, therefore, is, as it were, the substantial 'material cause' of our living being. It enables the soul – inasmuch as the soul informs a body and makes a complex living being subsist – to be visible, divisible, and measurable, to manifest itself in complexity, and to imply different capacities for 'moving itself.' The vital operations of the soul can be measured through and thanks to the body. They possess a biological life susceptible to external observation, while the soul can only be grasped in itself by the intellect, either inductively or affectively.

There is true philosophical knowledge of the living being when we

2 Plato, *Phaedrus*, 250c.

discover its radical principle: the soul. Otherwise there is only a descriptive and exterior knowledge of the living being, a knowledge that risks – whenever it claims to be the sole knowledge – making the living being material, because it no longer grasps what is most original. This is all the more striking because such knowledge by mensuration has developed considerably today, thanks to the perfecting of different instruments. This type of knowledge helps us to discover the extreme complexity of the living being, and its surprising organic unity. And so we are fascinated by a marvelous spectacle which manifests admirable order and astonishing harmony – whereas philosophical knowledge always remains very 'poor,' that is, less spectacular. Philosophical knowledge is knowledge which tends toward contemplation, knowledge which never seeks to dominate. It cannot engender power and so cannot tyrannize. It is a wholly qualitative knowledge, which seeks to 'listen' to the living being. Consequently, such knowledge remains fragile. The knowledge of our soul at the philosophical level – qualitative as it may be – remains knowledge that we do not perfectly possess, because of its difficulty. To use Aristotle's expression,[3] before the grasp of what is primary – such as our soul – our intellect is like the eyes of bats before the blaze of day. Yet we must maintain that such fragile knowledge really does attain to the soul, in its depth, as the principle of life; while scientific knowledge, seductive as it may be, cannot penetrate to the soul as the principle of life. Scientific knowledge grasps the effects, the 'fruits,' the order, the harmony that it brings about in the body; but it cannot say what the soul is in itself – that is to say, the principle and cause of life. It only measures its effects – which it cannot even consider as effects; it only grasps them as manifestations of life.

After discovering the soul as the radical principle of life, the philosopher must recognize that the human soul is the source of various degrees of life. It is easy enough to notice great diversity in our vital operations – from breathing and eating to thought, *cogito*. We can discern a hierarchy among these operations, some more dependent upon the body, more rooted in it, others more free. Some are more bound to physical becoming and quantitative juxtaposition, others are far more immanent and increasingly free of such juxtaposition.

What is certain is that, as distinguished from physical becoming, vital operation implies immanence. This is even what characterizes a vital operation. This immanence, however, is more or less victorious

3 Aristotle, *Metaphysics*, α, 1, 993b 9–11.

over the opaqueness of matter, and over the exteriority and juxtaposition of quantity. We thereby discern three major degrees of life: the *vegetative* life, the *sensitive* life, and the life *of the spirit*. Vegetative life remains most rooted in the organic body. The immanence of the operations of vegetative life is manifest in assimilation, the characteristic mode of a living being; but vegetative life always remains subject to the conditions of time and place. Sensitive life is life in which the phenomena of knowledge and passions appear, but it still remains *determined* by the organic body. The immanence of the operations of sensitive life is manifest in 'intentional[4] assimilation': in knowing the other, we 'become' it, yet without destroying it. Finally, the life of the spirit is the most immanent life. It is only *conditioned* by the organic body. The immanence of the operations of the life of the spirit is manifest in the self-lucidity of the judgment of existence. We are capable of respecting the other as we name it. It has its own meaning.

It seems important to maintain a distinction between three degrees of life. Aristotle made this distinction with great precision and it had already been grasped at the practical level by the Pythagoreans. It allows the discernment of an entire structure in the development of man's life. On the one hand, there is a structure at the base: the

---

4 The word 'intentional' – or 'intentionality,' the formalization of intentional: that whereby the intentional is intentional – used later regarding vegetative life (footnote 5 on p. 58), sensation (pp. 61–64), and intellectual knowledge (p. 76), is used at each level of life. Its meaning varies according to the level, but, each time, it arises with the distinction between being and life in all the realities that we experience. This distinction implies that, in certain cases, a living being, because of its life, because it is alive, is capable of anticipating what it will be in its perfection (as a living being), a perfection where the distance between being and life will be, as it were, resorbed. Intentionality expresses this anticipation. Thus a seed, a fetus, implies the anticipation of a perfectly determined living being. A moral intention is the anticipation, in a voluntary act, of the union of man to his end. The sensible intentional form is an anticipation, in sensation, of the sensible quality, which is itself ordered to the vegetative life in animals and immediately ordered to the judgment of existence or the judgment of contemplation in intelligent beings. As to an intelligible intentional form, it is an immediate anticipation of the adhesion of the intellect to existent reality. This clearly shows that we cannot stop at the intentional. We can and must distinguish it from reality; yet we cannot separate it if we want to remain in a realistic perspective. Intentionality shows the possibility that we have of enclosing ourselves in a form of immanence of vital operation and therefore of isolating ourselves from reality. This is erroneous since intentionality is essentially ordered to reality.

It would be interesting to see the connection between the immanence of vital operation and what we called the interiority of our vital operations. Immanence founds interiority. Interiority expresses a particular degree of immanence which appears with consciousness.

vegetative life with its own end. This life, common to all the living beings that we experience, is the *foundation* of our human life. On the other hand, there is the *summit* of our human life: the life of the spirit, whereby we discover what is ultimate in human life, and its own development, which is unique among all the living beings that we experience. The summit possesses its own organic structure. The development of this life cannot be isolated from its base. It depends upon it in its exercise while being independent of it in its proper specification and end.

There is also an intermediate life between the base and the summit: our sensitive life – sensations, imagination, passions – which is the connection (a reciprocal connection) between the vegetative and instinctive life and the spiritual life. This explains the complexity of our psychical life and its influence on our biological organs and on our intellectual and affective life. This 'third force,' so to speak, does not have a proper end. It is essentially anarchic; it can develop in various ways: it can be completely polarized by our instincts or, on the contrary, be totally assumed by our intellectual, amicable, and contemplative spiritual life.

Let us briefly analyze these various degrees of the life of man.

VEGETATIVE LIFE

The vegetative life has something very particular. It implies perfect homogeneous development and radical growth in the sense that it begins with the first moment of conception, and continues until man reaches the summit of his biological life. There is then a pause, followed by a diminution or decrease until death.

The first hidden, underground development – which modern genetic science has allowed us to discover in a remarkable way – shows how a living being is rooted in another living being, in its mother, and progressively develops in a *sui generis* way from this maternal source until the moment when, capable of vital autonomy, it detaches itself. This vegetative life is common to man and other animals – with extremely diverse modes and very different rhythms (think about the gestation of an elephant, for example). This first underground development shows the extent to which vegetative life and fertility are naturally bound together. There is an impressive vital continuity between an embryo and its maternal source, to such an extent that if separated from its source it can no longer develop harmoniously or even live. It is indeed totally dependent upon its vital milieu which

nourishes it and enables it to live. There is, as it were, a common
rhythm of life. Yet there is a new being, distinct from its maternal
source. The sign of this is that, from the first moment of its conception,
this new being, this living being, however small and fragile it may be,
is already the carrier of its own 'cipher,' different from that of its
mother and father. It already virtually has its 'program' of development.[5] It already is, in 'promise,' what it will be at its birth. If, during
the course of the first intra-uterine development, a living being is
completely dependent upon the rhythm of its vital milieu, its maternal
milieu – all the while possessing its autonomy and proper structure – it
then knows a fragility which renders it extraordinarily vulnerable. It is
in a state of unique receptivity.

A new phase of development begins at birth. The living being is
thenceforth autonomous in its life. It begins to breathe by itself (it
needs a new vital milieu which provides it with oxygen) and to feed on
maternal milk. The mother, therefore, continues to be its source of
nourishment. She is no longer the source of life in a radical (co-
substantial) way, but she is so in another way (through food). Does not
maternal milk have unique connaturality with the little baby?

Here is the first operation of the living being, an operation which
characterizes the vegetative life: it breathes and it eats. It is capable of
assimilating nutriment (oxygen and maternal milk) and transforming
it into its own biological life in order to grow and compensate for the
losses of energy caused by its struggles. For although the milieu in
which it lives furnishes its nourishment, certain noxious influences and
aggressive exterior forces also oppose it, for the milieu is not perfectly
adapted to its individuality. Thus it is simultaneously instinctively
attracted to the milieu and opposed to and defensive towards it. A
balance must be sought in order to live.

Moreover, in breathing and nourishing itself, a living being absorbs
toxic elements that it cannot assimilate and thus rejects, transforming
into itself only those it can assimilate. There is also a struggle at the
internal level, for a separation necessarily takes place between what is

---

5 We can affirm in an absolute way that there is a new being only if we can affirm
that the soul is created at conception, as the soul is the principle of being. We
cannot affirm this however, for we cannot know at exactly what moment the soul is
created. We only have a demonstration by means of sign. We are familiar with the
objection of some: a fetus is not a human person. To this we reply that this cannot
be concluded in a categorical fashion one way or the other. A fetus, in its living
being, is virtually, 'intentionally,' a human person. In its being, it is totally, vitally
(really) ordered to man. Its perfect being is none other than that of man. By
destroying it, therefore, I destroy the man intentionally present in it.

transformed into the organic body and what is rejected. From its outset, biological life develops within struggle, a struggle which lasts throughout its development, with moments of blossoming, and moments of crisis when the operations of breathing and eating can no longer be perfectly lived; these operations are indispensable for biological life. A living being endowed with a biological life cannot continue if it does not breathe and eat.

These fundamental operations permit growth. An infant must develop according to the demands of its individual nature. In its rhythm of growth, there may be pauses and obstacles. This is normal, for biological life takes place in struggle. There is also a particularly important moment in this development, that of puberty. A perfect living being is capable of engendering and procreating. Puberty marks the passage from the still imperfect state of a living being incapable of fecundity to the perfect state of a living being capable of fecundity. A profound mutation occurs, and the sexual instinct develops and manifests itself.

After reaching its summit, and staying for some time at this level, man's vegetative life experiences a period of decline which leads to death. True, a living being as living being is not ordered to death; but the individual experiences a decline, i.e., old age, where the weight of matter prevails and the unity of the living being is no longer as strong. Division enters into the living being until the most radical division occurs: the separation of soul and body.

Before dying, however, man, as a living being, has normally procreated. The act of procreation, for the purpose of the survival of the human species, can only occur in cooperation between a man and a woman. This act gives the difference of the sexes its deep meaning. The superior living being is too imperfect to be the source of life and fecundity by itself. It must experience the cooperation of another who is instinctively and biologically adapted to such complementarity, complementarity not only at the organic level but also at the level of instinctive sexual appetite. The two are instinctively and biologically made for each other, male and female, for the purpose of fecundity, the survival of the species.

While the instincts of respiration and nutrition are at the level of the individual and are expressed in the radical egoism of a living being struggling to live, the sexual instinct, the instinct for procreation, is at the level of the species and its survival. That is why it is so deeply rooted in the individual; in a certain sense, it surpasses and imposes itself upon it.

If we philosophically analyze the specific character of these two instincts – the instinct for breathing and eating, and the sexual instinct – we come to recognize their deep, radical distinction, their proper ends. If we only consider their exercise, we can no longer distinguish their proper character, and they seem to intermingle, to interpenetrate. Their distinction, however, does not prohibit there being an order between the two. Individual instinct at the level of nutriment is ordered to sexual instinct, as the individual is ordered to the species. Procreation is the end, and thus brings to completion the vegetative life. As the ancients used to say, 'Only one who is perfect can engender.' Procreation gives biological life its ultimate meaning. Consequently, if assimilation is the fundamental characteristic of a living being endowed with vegetative life, fecundity is the end of this living being, is what brings it to completion. It is fulfilled in surpassing itself, in ceding its place to another who is its fruit and thus enables it to survive – not in itself, but in progeny of the same species. Certain Greek philosophers saw in this an 'imitation' of eternity. Might there be a kind of intention of eternity in species? There is surely something in species that is beyond time.

Procreation ends in a new living being of the same species. A mother gives birth to a child, a 'son of man' who, despite its dependence upon its milieu, is metaphysically a human person with autonomy of life and being. This little human child has a spiritual soul. Whence does it come? Is it communicated to it by its parents? Does it come from without? We cannot answer at the level of vegetative life. But what we can say is that a living being which reproduces transmits life similar to its own. That is why the one who is born has the same life as the one who is the source of its life. Procreation does not imply the degradation or loss of life. This is true of all living beings. A grain of wheat is the source of another grain of wheat of the same species, and even the source of a multitude of grains of wheat. There is a marvelous superabundance of life in such reproduction. We find something similar at the level of man's fecundity: a single spermatozoon becomes fertile when it encounters an ovule, but millions of others could have become so. Why this superabundance? At first glance, it seems a luxury, a waste, even uselessness, and could lead one to conclude that there is, at that moment, a suspension of end or purpose which leaves everything to chance. On the contrary, however, it makes the survival of the species more sure, and thus assures the end more perfectly. And is this not to help us grasp better how life surpasses matter? Life, while engaged in matter, is victorious over it; and this is manifest at the very moment of its gift. Life is transmitted with superabundance. Matter, on the contrary, contracts and limits. Is matter not the source of chance?

This superabundance of life in its fecundity is in order that life may be victorious over chance and impose its proper end.

SENSITIVE LIFE

SENSATIONS

We have no consciousness of vegetative life in itself. Although we know its effects, we do not clearly grasp the 'whatness' of respiration, nutrition, or procreation. We can discover the laws of their conditioning, but what they are deeply escapes us. When a father and mother beget a child they do not know what procreation is; they do not know what this natural and fundamental operation is, what this substantial operation is. Although they can desire and wish to have a child and, for this, do everything that nature requires for their union to produce its fruit, they cannot, strictly speaking, choose the individuality or the sex of their child. In reality, they do not command nature. Although they have power over the exercise of procreation, their sexual union, they do not have power over the determination nor the end of this vital operation – no more than over their respiration and nutrition. They can modify certain conditions of exercise – the choice of foods, the rhythm of meals, to some extent the rhythm of breathing – but they cannot modify the specific character of these operations; they are naturally determined.

On the other hand, we can have a deeper consciousness of the vital exercise of our sensations and passions, thanks to the intervention of our willed, or voluntary, attentiveness. I can be careful to observe, to see, to hear. I can let myself be carried away by a particular passion. Here is a new intervention of the life of our spirit which assumes the vital activity of sensitive knowledge and can live it, as it were, from within. This is what psychology calls 'perception.' Our purpose here is not to describe our consciousness of this vital activity; Merleau-Ponty has already done this very well.[6] We wish, however, to try to analyze it, to discern its various elements. There is reflexive consciousness of sensation, but such consciousness is not the sensation considered in itself, for we can have reflexive consciousness of a tactile sensation, an auditory sensation, a dream, an affective state, etc. We must, therefore, try to specify – in philosophical analysis – the originality of each of the sensations, that is, vision, touch, etc.

My consciousness of seeing and hearing – a consciousness which

6 Maurice Merleau-Ponty, *Phenomenology of Perception.*

indeed allows me to experience the joy of seeing a particular sight and hearing a particular harmonious sound – is not exterior but immanent to the sensation. But it does not determine it or specify it. It does not reveal to us, therefore, the proper character of sensation; however, it does allow us to observe it in a privileged way, as it were 'from within.' We are not merely a choice spectator. We live the sensation. Thus at the level of vital exercise there is profound unity between a particular sensation and our consciousness of it – precisely why, in phenomenological reflection, one stops at the description of perceptions.

Let us ask the following question from a philosophical viewpoint: What is a sensation? What is such-and-such (a) sensation? What is *my* vision of *this* rose? Sensation is the most immediate vital operation of knowledge. When I see a tree, a rose, or the sky, I sense; I have a very particular contact with a sensible reality. This contact is particular in that it modifies the one who senses, sees, knows, yet changes nothing of the reality sensed, seen and known. The scarlet rose, for example, is not modified whether I look at it alone or whether ten people look at it at the same time as I. Such is not the case, however, if I touch it and ten other people touch it; it can lose its brilliance, and wilt. From this viewpoint there is a great difference between the two types of sensitive knowledge: seeing and touching (we shall come back to this). Let us first specify the nature of sight. Sight modifies me and does not modify the seen reality. Sight is, therefore, no longer a phenomenon of the purely physical order but of another order: that of sensitive knowledge. Such knowledge is totally dependent upon the real presence of the seen reality; sight ceases if the reality disappears. Hence a living being that sees does not have autonomy in the order of the specification, the determination of the seen reality; it only has autonomy in the order of exercise, in that it applies itself to seeing and does not close its eyes. This is the first moment of realism as regards knowledge. The determination of our knowledge remains totally dependent upon that which is seen. This is indeed true of all sensations. Thus we can say that sight allows us to 'become' – at a very particular level – not the various seen realities, strictly speaking, but their various colors, their figure, their movement; everything that is immediately visible. When we say what the seen reality is, we are no longer at the level of sight. Another knowledge allows us to say what the reality is. Sight immediately grasps (a particular) color – in fact, sight grasps light in the first place, as hearing grasps (a particular) sound.

In line with this, notice that certain 'sensibles' are grasped by more than one sense (common sensibles): movement and magnitude (or size) for example, can be seen (we see a reality moving), heard (we hear a reality approaching), and/or touched. Other sensibles, on the contrary, are only grasped by a single sense (proper sensibles): light and color are only grasped by sight; cold and hot are only grasped by touch; sound only by hearing, etc. In this way Aristotle distinguishes 'proper sensibles' from 'common sensibles.' The distinction is important, although it has been understood in different ways. For Aristotle, the objectivity of our sensations is ultimately based upon the 'proper sensibles.' Here, contact with existent reality is primary from the sensitive viewpoint. According to Descartes, however, the objectivity of our sensations is ultimately based upon the 'common sensibles,' because only these sensibles are directly measurable; the 'proper sensibles' are subjective because they are not measurable. From this we can distinguish two very different perspectives on the objectivity of sight. For Descartes, objectivity is reduced to what is measurable. According to Aristotle, objectivity is primarily qualitative. Quality is what is most determined and most actual in reality; quality is what first specifies our sight.

Thus, through sight we 'become,' in an immanent fashion, at the level of sensitive knowledge, the 'proper sensibles' of color and light. What does this 'becoming' mean? It is no longer of the physical order, but of a new order which has traditionally been called 'intentional' – in other words, an order which is completely relative to another and yet exists with its own determination, structure, and form. In seeing, I *intentionally* become the colors seen. There is a 'beyond' to the measurable, physical world, a 'beyond' which nevertheless remains immediately dependent upon the same existent, physical world.

This 'intentional' contact with, and dependence upon, the physical world are particularly clear in the case of touch. Touch entails sensitive knowledge. Through touch I know hot and I know cold; I intentionally become (this) hot or cold, yet this knowledge also physically modifies the touched reality. There is a certain reciprocity between the intentional and the physical because of the immediate contact with the sensed reality required by touch. Thus there is a distinction, but not a separation, between the physical and the intentional, because there can be interdependence.

Let us try to specify further what this intentional becoming is. It is a becoming because a change is brought about in the one who sees. It is necessary, then, that the one who sees possesses a capacity for being acted upon by 'sensibles' (both proper and common). All becoming presupposes a potentiality; all vital becoming presupposes a vital receptivity, a capacity for being determined and, at the same time, for vitally reacting, exercising itself, 'operating.' A potentiality is necessary, therefore, in the intentional order, a receptivity and, at the same time, a capacity for operating or acting. These are according to the sensible intentional order, for this becoming is an immanent operation occurring in the living being, the one who sees. This capacity for being determined and acting is what we call a vital power (δυναμισ *dunamis*). If I philosophically analyze sight, I discover it to be an 'intentional assimilation' which presupposes a present seen reality (this reality, in its visible aspect, specifies and determines sight). Sight also presupposes, in the living being which sees, a power which involves both a receptivity and a capacity for moving itself, a capacity for exercising a vital operation in an immanent fashion.

The immanence of the vital operation here is much more intimate than in respiration and nutrition because it overcomes the opaqueness of physical and material becoming. There is an intentional assimilation which brings about a unity with that which is seen – the sensible – without destroying it and reducing it to the living being, but, rather, respecting its proper determinations. In gazing upon a rose I become its color and I respect its proper quality. This sensitive knowledge is characterized by the fact that it does not occur in struggle, for it is beyond physical becoming; indeed, it implies a more intimate immanence than that of nutrition. This immanence is, so to speak, a pure, limitless immanence which can be source of joy; its only limit is that of the conditioning of the physical organ it presupposes, an organ that cannot bear certain overly intense sensible extremes, because such extremes risk impairing it. The conditioning of the physical organ also impedes our sensations from always being exercised, precisely because a physical organ tires.

It would be good to review for ourselves the diversity and the proper character of the five senses, with the understanding that the sense of touch is the most fundamental. Touch is the most realistic sense and best shows the continuity and the distinction between the physical universe and the intentional order. Touch is the sense of life *par excellence*. Sight, on the other hand, is the ultimate sense, the sense most free with respect to the physical universe, the sense which can embrace the horizon, the firmament, in its expanse. Sight is the sense of light, the most spiritual and most qualitative sensible.

IMAGINATIVE REPRESENTATIONS

Our sensations are prolonged in representations which give us the realm of images. If I close my eyes after looking at the scarlet of a rose,

I form within myself an 'image' which re-presents the scarlet of the rose. This is a new type of knowledge – sensitive, yet not the sensation of external senses. This new sensitive knowledge which forms images is no longer an intentional assimilation; it is a sort of growth or extension of our sensations and, at the same time, a sort of synthesis of what was seen, heard, touched, etc. This sensitive knowledge re-presents what was seen, heard, or touched and grasps it in an entirely new way, its own way. It creates images. What is curious and astonishing is that these interior, sensitive images entail both the proper and common sensibles, but in reverse order. The common sensibles are re-presented first in an image, whereas the proper sensibles are re-presented in a relative way. We are in the presence of a synthesis that re-presents, in an original way, what was previously sensed.

If we philosophically analyze images, asking what they are and where they come from, we discover that they are sensitive 'intentional forms' capable of re-presenting. They are the first syntheses of knowledge – in the sensible order. They are syntheses whose source is in us. Consequently, they are not properly objective but primarily a subjective synthesis, with, nevertheless, a basis in reality. We must, therefore, posit a particular power as the source of these images, the power we call the imagination. The imagination can only be exercised from our external senses, and thus it is moved. Yet it also moves itself; it is a source of new knowledge whose proper fruit is an image.

What characterizes this knowledge, apart from its synthetic character, is its autonomy; it is no longer immediately dependent upon reality. We can develop an imaginary world within us which, by itself, has no limits, which is infinite in potentiality and development.

This knowledge, precisely because it is limitless in its development, has no proper end; it can be utilized in various ways. It is essentially like the intersection of various vital operations. The intellect and the will can make use of the imagination in many ways. Our passions can also make use of it. And our instincts can ally themselves with it. As a matter of fact, the images used by our intellect and will, passions and instincts form the fabric of our psyche; and in this complex fabric different levels can be distinguished. There is conscious psyche, with clear images at the service of intellectual, volitional, and passional activities. There is pre-conscious psyche, psyche based upon vague images, the psyche of natural appetites and fundamental aspirations which incline towards certain imprecise goals. Pre-conscious psyche itself involves different zones. We should probably discern between a fundamental, unconscious zone which stems from the radical potentiality of instincts, and more determined zones (certain determinations having already been given) which, however, remain unconscious relative to clear consciousness. The latter is the zone of customary dispositions, of already established orientations, habits, and conditioned reflexes.

Finally, we should discern a zone that arises from what has been repressed, from misunderstandings suffered, the violence of the external milieu, all that has frustrated and arrested natural affective élans, or has provoked inner turbulence and bitterness, and forced withdrawal because it hinders the expression of desires and aspirations. Here we should acknowledge where Freud is correct in what he says of the subconscious. There may be deep subconscious zones, especially if our repressions come from the earliest moments of our youth. There may be a zone which is no longer 'pre-conscious,' a zone that arises from a consciousness that has suffered violence and thus falls to an 'unconscious' level, awaiting the right moment to manifest itself, to explode – like a stick of dynamite of which one is no longer conscious. From a philosophical viewpoint, this subconscious zone is never primary. It is always secondary. It is the result of certain repressions and is always at the level of conditioning. Thus we cannot explain who man is with primary reference to his subconscious. Such an explanation was Freud's philosophical error.

We see the importance – and the difficulty – of philosophical inquiry into the realm of images. This realm places us in the presence of a new immanence of our vital operations: our imagination creates images within itself; it creates its own imaginative syntheses apart from the realities of the physical world. Man can distance himself thereby from the physical world. He becomes capable of retiring into himself and isolating himself, building a new, purely imaginative universe within himself. Is not this the imagination's glory and, at the same time, its redoubtable power? It is able to turn us away from the existent realities of our universe and dazzle our eyes with a new universe of which it is the source.

In continuity with the imagination, and still in the realm of images, is *memory*. A living being endowed with sensitive life is not content with sensing or imagining. It keeps the images it has formed in order to make use of them on appropriate occasions. Memory is prodigious, for it enables a living being endowed with sensitive life to emerge beyond the succession of time and have a certain interior duration. While procreation manifests that the species of a living being is beyond time, the memory of a living being endowed with sensitive life shows how the individual seeks to go beyond the parceling out of time. Memory stems from the imagination and helps it develop, because it stocks past images; but it stocks them so that they can once again be actuated and associated with other new images. One might say that imagination innovates, and memory keeps and conserves. Here we see the appearance of two opposed tendencies in a living being at the level of sensitive knowledge: keeping and conserving, renewing and innovating. At the level of external sensation these two tendencies do not appear, for there a living being is relative to the actual presence of the existent realities of the universe. It is only thanks to the imagination that a living being begins to realize a certain synthesis, in greater immanence and autonomy, thereby acquiring greater independence with respect to others and a more acute sense of its distinction. But it then needs both more interior wealth and possession of the past.

Here it may be interesting to analyze what dreams are (those which appear in a state of sleep). Philosophically speaking, they are pure images, pure representations which remain conditioned by the milieu, but at the same time are, as it were, separated from their source (the sensations) and are no longer used by the intellect, thus escaping the intellectual consciousness of judgment. This gives them a mobility which allows them to develop spontaneously in many directions, the order of which we are not aware. Not knowing their order leaves the field wide open for different interpretations.

Do dreams come from our subconscious? Do they come from our different sensations, from the affectivity lived during the day? Do they portend what will happen? Are there premonitions or prophetic dreams? There is great interest in dreams today, but their analysis is perhaps too purely psychoanalytic. They should also be analyzed from a philosophical perspective in order to know better all man's complexity. This would be difficult from a Cartesian perspective, in which dreams are considered offal, that is, a waste. Freud's position was diametrically opposed to this. According to Freud, dreams reveal the subconscious, and the subconscious determines the psyche.

PASSIONS

Parallel to the various types of sensitive knowledge are our different sensitive appetites, our passional tendencies, which we readily experience and of which we are conscious. At times we experience affective '*élans*,' or movements, which carry us towards certain sensible realities that attract and allure us. These attractions can sometimes be very vehement and divert us from what we consider to be our duty.

However, we do not only experience attractions. We can also experience hatred, repulsion, and opposition, which affectively turn us away and urge us to distance ourselves from certain sensible evils. We can, in certain circumstances, also experience a violent anger that arouses a desire to break and destroy everything because we cannot bear an apparent disorder that wounds us in our sensitive affectivity, in our appetites. Such anger can seize us in a way that makes everything else seem to disappear momentarily. Seneca, in his treatise on anger, compares an angry person to certain enraged animals which hurl themselves upon what irritates them in order to destroy it.[7] Such impetuous, repulsive, or angry feelings do indeed seem very similar to those we see in other animals. An animal has an advantage, because its affective states ordinarily manifest themselves in an instinctive way, whereas in an adult human being they can be controlled so that nothing can be detected from the outside.

There can be powerful exaltations that lead to states of euphoria. On the other hand, there can also be states of depression, or sorrow, that make us withdraw completely. These affective states are part of the complexity of our psyche and, as we have indicated, they are often closely linked to our imaginative knowledge.

What are these affective states, these passional tendencies? Psychologists are very familiar with them and offer interesting and acute descriptions; but they do not analyze them philosophically. That is why they cannot really grasp either what they are or their specific diversity. They can only show their effects and their mutual reactions: for example, how a particular affective state is provoked by another, and how they can neutralize one another or, on the contrary, amplify one another.

If we want to know what these passional tendencies are, we must analyze them. They are certainly real. We cannot doubt their existence, for we experience them every day. Nevertheless, their reality is very particular, for they exist at the level of intentional sensitive affectivity. These passional tendencies come from us and remain in us, yet they are capable of modifying our biological life to the point of provoking grave disturbances.

Unlike the sensitive intentionality of the imagination – which is of the realm of knowledge and representation – the affective sensitive intentionality is an *élan*, an inclination towards another, towards a represented sensible good which attracts us, and can exert a force of irresistible attraction upon us. This affective intentionality is a dynamic

7 Seneca, *De Ira*, I, 1.

force which compels us to come out of ourselves; as we have seen, imaginative sensitive intentionality (which remains within us) does not do this.

A passional *élan* is always the fruit of the attraction of a sensible good sensitively represented; yet it is experienced in two different ways: either it is simply the fruit of the attraction of a sensible good or the fruit of the attraction of a difficult-to-acquire sensible good, an 'arduous' sensible good. With the latter, the passional *élan* involves a struggle. The attraction is no longer immediate; it presupposes a difficult struggle. Thus, at the level of the passions, we distinguish between the 'concupiscible' and the 'irascible,' the former being immediately specified by the attraction of a sensible good, the latter by the attraction, in struggle, of a difficult and arduous sensible good.

The first passion of the concupiscible is love, and with it are born desire and delight, or pleasure. Love is indeed the fundamental passion, the passion which immediately concerns the attraction of a known sensible good. This good, being known, awakens an attraction, a call, an *élan*. This attraction affectively 'connaturalizes' the one who loves with the good that he loves; it renders him 'proportionate' and affectively unites him with this good in a unity that is realized at the affective, sensible, intentional level. This passional, or passionate, love moves towards the known, sensible good. It makes the one who experiences it move outward toward something which is not himself, toward another, another as his good. In this sense passional love is 'ex-static.' This love also hollows out a capacity for welcome, for receptivity with respect to the loved good. By connaturalizing us with a loved good, passional love renders it present to us. We carry it within us and it gives us a new *'élan* for life' and new strength – and also a new capacity for suffering, for we become vulnerable to all that concerns this good.

Because this sensible good awakens in us this love-passion, we must sensitively know the good. Nevertheless, sensitive knowledge of the good is not what determines the passion. The former is specified by the sensible good itself. Knowledge is a necessary condition; it is at the service of the good that attracts and arouses the love.

When the loved sensible good is not possessed, the love it arouses remains imperfect, and then what we have is a desire, a call. Desire-passion is none other than an incipient love for an unpossessed sensible good. Love-passion is an affective union, a connaturalization of the person who loves with that which he loves. Desire-passion is an affective *élan*, an inclination, a thirst, a call: affectively, we tend wholly towards the good that we love but which eludes us, which we do not yet possess. This affective tension is capable of mobilizing all our energies with a view to possessing the good. A passional desire can be so vehement that it captivates our entire sensitive being, orienting it towards that which we seek to possess.

We affectively rest in the good when it is possessed; we enjoy it. Delight is this passional rest which makes blossom our sensitive affectivity in the possessed good.

There is a strong connection between these three passions, love, desire, and delight; that is why we can no longer distinguish them if we only consider the exercise of our vital operations. For love is, as it were, the proper source of desire, and desire is brought to completion in delight. If we analyze them philosophically, we can no longer say that they are simply three moments in the development of the same passion. For with regards to the known sensible good, possession or non-possession essentially modifies the relation of the sensible good to us, for a sensible good requires physical presence and contact. That is why non-possession is a privation. The sensible good is only fully itself when it is possessed. This explains how love-passion can be, in itself, so possessive and why it demands to possess the sensible good, and thus be brought to completion in delight.

Parallel to these passions for a sensible good are three passions for a sensible evil, three 'anti-loves.' In the presence of that which, from the sensible viewpoint, wounds us and hinders the blossoming of our sensitive affectivity – what we call sensible evil – we have a violent reaction: opposition. We flee in our affectivity. We turn away, or simply drown in sorrow if the evil overpowers us and seems victorious.

If we analyze these different 'negative' passions, we can distinguish three of them: hatred, flight (or aversion), and sadness (or sorrow).

Hatred is the passion aroused in us by sensible evil, that which is capable of affectively wounding us. Hatred is not a fundamental and primary passion. It always presupposes a passional love which, unable to blossom, is transformed into hatred; this is readily understood, for evil is never primary and fundamental. It is always the privation of a good. Evil is always relative to the good and is only known and attained in its reference to it. The passion of hatred is 'anti-love.' It is the negation and absolute rejection of what seems to be noxious and capable of hurting us. It is, at the sensitive level, a sort of affective annihilation. Hatred-passion places us in a state of enmity, of sensitive affective opposition to that which presents itself as our enemy, as capable of harming us. It places us in an affective state of refusal, of negation, unlike love-passion which connaturalizes us with the good by placing us in an affective state of receptivity.

If the evil does not yet seem to be present, but is imagined as imminent though not yet arrived, hatred will then be the source of a passional flight which affectively places us as far away as possible, diverting us from the imminent evil; we seek to affectively distance ourselves. This is a sort of antithesis of desire. The passion of flight is really a reverse *élan*: we turn our backs on the imminent sensible evil. The passion of flight inhibits us affectively; it compels us to hide within ourselves in order to find shelter and refuge far from the evil which may occur.

If the sensible evil is present and we have the impression that it is overcoming us and can crush or vanquish us in our sensitive being, sadness grips and envelops us; the more the sensible evil seems to be victorious, the more sadness seizes and oppresses us. Unlike joy, which dilates us, sadness grabs us by the throat and forces us to withdraw, affectively suppressing all blossoming. Removing all expansion, it not only affectively 'knocks us out,' but, when deeply rooted in our sensitive affectivity, it also leaves us exhausted, as if annihilated. For then evil is triumphant and there is no escape. The death of a friend whom we loved exclusively, from the viewpoint of passional delight, can provoke such sadness. There is no longer any escape for us who remain alone; we remain in our sadness, like a hunted animal.

If the passion of hatred presupposes the passion of love, we must recognize that there can be a transition from love to hatred. Must we then admit that love-passion implies in itself a certain ambivalence, as some psychologists claim? This seems accurate at the level of the exercise and conditioning of the passions, because the sensible good is not absolute; it has limits, and the transition from limit to privation is not impossible. However, at the philosophical level, love-passion is not ordered to hatred-passion. The latter presupposes love-passion, in much the same way that evil presupposes good. There is ambivalence in the sense that evil presupposes good, but not in the sense that good and evil are correlative and 'summon' each other.

If the passion of hatred presupposes that of love, can we say that the passion of flight equally presupposes that of desire, and that sadness presupposes delight? We cannot establish this, because there is not a rigorous parallel between the presence and absence of good and the presence and absence of evil. Besides, although evil presupposes good, the closeness of evil does not necessarily presuppose the closeness of good. Consider the arousal of the passion of flight, for example, which presupposes an awareness of the presence of evil. I may very well be aware of an imminent evil without being aware of the imminence of the good the evil presupposes. Thus the passion of flight presupposes the passion of love, but not necessarily that of desire. We can make the same analysis of sadness in relation to delight: delight may have existed before sadness, but nevertheless we normally have a more acute awareness of the sadness; while it necessarily presupposes love, sadness does not necessarily presuppose delight.

The irascible passions can be analyzed in the same way. An arduous, sensible good, known through sensation and the imagination, arouses in us the passion of audacity. We aspire to be united with the difficult good. We rush headlong towards it with all our sensitive strength. This passion presupposes a love for the sensible good; but because this good is difficult and arduous, love is not enough. It is transformed into the passion of audacity.

If the difficult sensible good is absent, it arouses in us a passion of hope which, in contrast to desire, is not only an *élan*, a call, but a force of conquest: we do not hesitate to orient all our vital energies towards the unpossessed, difficult, sensible good. And when this difficult sensible good is possessed, we enjoy it. The concupiscible love-passion is thus the source of these two irascible passions, and the passion of delight is their term. The irascible is carried by the passion of love and is brought to completion in the passion of delight; the irascible is therefore enveloped by the concupiscible.

When a difficult-to-overcome evil appears to us as such, the passion of audacity is transformed into the passion of fear: we fear the violent evil, this evil which appears powerful. We know how fear, or dread, is distinguished from anxiety. The former involves a determined sensible evil able to attack us – we fear the enormous dog which has attacked us before – while anxiety is an affective inhibition which immerses us in ourselves in a radical and total way. With anxiety, there is no longer a precise and determined motive. It involves, as it were, forgetting the initial experience which awakened fear and dread in us. The imagination seizes the affective state of withdrawal.

An imminent difficult-to-overcome evil arouses in us the passion of despair which saps all our strength. This passion destroys the passion of hope. It involves affective withdrawal which, unlike flight, is a much deeper and more radical withdrawal which totally disarms us and makes us capable of delivering ourselves affectively and sensitively to the evil, to the enemy: the enemy is there, it is useless to struggle; he has us beaten.

Finally, when a present sensible evil violently shatters someone we love, and we consider ourselves able to thrust aside the sensible evil and reject it, we become angry. The passion of anger is a complex passion, the most noble passion, the passion closest to our intellect. A present evil, an evil which we want to reject in order to re-establish the good which it has shattered, awakens anger in us. When the anger is truly profound, the good is a certain visible and sensible order of justice. It is harmony in the realities and the people that surround us and form our milieu. Anger seeks to stop disorder and restore the first order – or at least what appears, to our sensitive and imaginative knowledge linked to our practical intellect, to be a state of disorder in comparison to the previous order that we loved, an order that we ourselves or those whom we love had established. We seek to defend the order and the first harmony we love; and when it seems that someone is in the process of destroying it, we hasten to restore it and prevent it from being damaged. Anger has a unique, sensitive, affective violence; it can increase our energy tenfold, for our affectivity suddenly finds itself, as it were, in a state of ebulliance that can no longer be contained within the normal limits of our ordinary conditioning, the limits of day-to-day relations in communal life. That is why anger suddenly shatters with violence what appears to engender disorder. Having been contained for a time, anger-passion sometimes explodes with even more force, like a thunderbolt in the thick and dark obscurity of clouds. Someone who is angry is no longer in control of himself; he is completely overcome by a force that seeks to save the present sensible good which is in the process of foundering and being destroyed before his eyes. Yet anger can also be a cry of distress, the cry of someone who, for one last time, engages everything in order not to let the good which he loves be destroyed.

Political anger gives rise to a revolutionary spirit; hatred and despair, on the other hand, give birth more to a spirit of anarchy which destroys for the sake of destroying. Anger destroys in the hope of freeing the alienated man from the tyrant.

With the passions we remain in an affective, intentional, sensitive becoming, a becoming which, in a certain sense, has no end, for passions summon one another and also oppose themselves to one another. Indeed, while a passion is indeed 'being acted upon,' it is also a reaction; all this occurs in our psyche, in the immanence of our passional operations. In some passions, the sensitive 'being acted upon' dominates, while in others the reaction dominates (think of love and anger, for example) and then we find ourselves in the midst, so to speak, of a storm on a lake with a whirlwind of different passions. Our passions never cease to be in movement and agitation. Nevertheless, in their incessant whirlwind we can discern, as it were, different summits. These summits are not, however, ends in the precise sense; for passions, in and of themselves, although specified by sensible goods, do not find their end in them. Through his passions, man loves the sensible good for his own sake. He himself is the ultimate end of passional love, yet passions give him no real rest; they keep him in agitation.

The passion of anger is a summit; it is the apex of all the irascible passions and can give them ultimate meaning. In comparison, delight and sadness are the ends of the concupiscible passions: everything is brought to completion either in sadness or in delight. The passion of love is a hidden source. Hate is an 'anti-source'; it can poison our sensitivity by turning it in on itself.

We see how the imagination, with its many recesses, can nourish our affective passional states, making us pass successively from one passion to another, and keeping us in a 'tragic' state if our irascible is very developed, or in a depressive state of sadness and despair if our irascible has been vanquished.

We can add that man, a living being endowed with sensitive life, is capable of moving himself; he is capable of locomotion. He has a vital power whereby he dominates the conditioning of the place in which he finds himself. If he moves about, it is above all to nourish himself, to find a vital milieu where he is best able to develop, and avoid what can harm him. Most of the time the passions of desire, flight, anger, and hate motivate and color his movements. And his different passions manifest themselves in how he moves; obviously, someone who is moved by the desire to nourish himself does not move in the same way as someone moved by fear, or flight, to avoid a dangerous animal. Someone moved by anger does not behave in the same way as someone possessed by hatred. The passions incarnate themselves in man's gait and behavior.[8]

THE LIFE OF THE SPIRIT

Beyond the vegetative life and the sensitive life is the life of the spirit, that of the intellect and the will. Our experience in our human life –

8 The biological sciences and experimental psychology have thoroughly analyzed material causality and the dispositions of the vital movements of locomotion, action, and reaction to the vital milieu, or environment, in which man finds himself. If we want to carry this philosophical study further, we must take these analyses into account by placing them at their level of research of the 'how,' which helps us to grasp better how man, a living being endowed with sensitive life, locally moves himself and reacts to his milieu.

because we are conscious of it – is that, at certain moments, we think, we reflect, we stop working manually in order to meditate. We also judge or criticize what we are doing and what we see around us. We make decisions: for example, we change our life or do a particular project. Beyond our work and our practical decisions there is a spiritual appetite, a will, which is their source.

Let us analyze these various activities philosophically. What characterizes them is primarily their transcendence with respect to the body, the immediate sensible realm, imaginative representations, and, lastly, the passions. These activities allow us to enter a new realm of the intimate knowledge of reality and its meaning. We 'read' reality from within (*intelligere* = *intus legere*). We then grasp what the different experienced realities are and can reflect upon their meaning in itself, beyond the circumstances of time and place in which the sensible realities exist, beyond the *hic et nunc*, the here and now. We are able to affirm the existence of a particular experienced and sensed reality, as beyond us and apart from us. We can discover proper principles and establish laws (the constant relations of anteriority and posteriority between facts). In so doing, becoming is surpassed. Indeed, we are capable of reaching 'that-which-is.' It is here that we grasp what truly characterizes the life of our spirit.

Our volitional, or voluntary, acts are capable of attaining a spiritual good, that is, a human person, a friend, which is capable of arousing love within us.

Thus these vital operations are more independent from our body than the sensations and the passions. What determines them is no longer a physical, sensible reality, but something real beyond the sensible: 'that-which-is,' principles, a spiritual good. These vital operations, therefore, have a deeper autonomy and immanence than vital operations at the sensitive level, for they not only emanate from a living being (as do all vital operations), and have their own forms at the intentional level (as do sensations and passions); they also have their own end. While sensitive life is anarchic by nature, because it has no proper end, the life of the spirit, on the contrary, has an end. Unlike the vegetative life which also has, in a certain sense, a proper end – although only in the survival of the species through the intermediary of a new living being of which it is the source – the life of the spirit allows man, in his individuality as man, to reach a spiritual good able to be his end and complete him and thereby render him happy. Such happiness occurs thanks to the full blossoming of his personality. Here we discover the proper nobility and the unique perfection of the life of the spirit. In man, the life of the spirit does radically depend upon the vegetative life and, in a more direct way, upon the sensitive life; yet it has its own autonomy and independence, because it has its own end.

In order to understand this better we must distinguish, in the various operations of our spiritual life, those which are of the realm of knowledge from those which are of the realm of volitional affectivity.

KNOWLEDGE

As regards knowledge, the vital operation of the spirit – which manifests itself most immediately – is our reflection upon our reasoning, which, in fact, takes on different forms. Reasoning involves a certain vital immanent becoming; it indeed occurs within ourselves, in our mind. What we seek to do in reasoning is to grasp the different relations that can be established in the diversity of our prior knowledge. A certain interior movement then occurs, a movement which is a true spiritual becoming and of which we are the immediate source. And there we discover the vitality of our spirit, our reason. The mind is able to move itself and progress, for the purpose of reasoning is to acquire new knowledge. Unlike physical movement, the growth of living beings, and even becoming at the level of images, this 'rational becoming' does not occur in juxtaposition and quantitative exteriority but in the immanence of spiritual knowledge. This immanence, however, does not do away with true becoming or true progress. Like all becoming, this becoming presupposes contraries and a subject. It certainly reveals the radical potentiality of our reason and its capacity for bringing itself to completion and determining itself. And this determination occurs from within: the reasoning mind actuates itself by making use of what it already has within itself. It is both the subject of this becoming – and so necessarily involves a certain potentiality – and its immanent source. In reasoning the mind grasps that certain oppositions help it to discover something new which was previously veiled and hidden.

In fact, this unveiling occurs in reasoning which involves a syllogism, that is to say, two propositions united or joined together with a view to a 'common work': the inference of a conclusion. Compared with the first propositions, there is a true unveiling. For example: the soul is the principle of life of a living being. Now every principle of life is prior to that which comes from it (vital operations, the informing of the organic body). Thus the soul is prior ...

This development can also be done in an inductive fashion. From different, multiple realities which nevertheless have something in common, we discover the source of the unity in diversity. The unveiling is completely different from the previous one, for it is the discovery of a source, not a property, which is a secondary reality.

Finally, there is an unveiling done according to a procedure of opposition. This procedure entails denying what was affirmed in the first place in order to discover what is radically common beyond the opposition. This procedure is a dialectical approach, of the type often encountered today. It is an old procedure, but one used in antiquity at the artistic level, especially in rhetoric. Since Fichte, Schelling, and Hegel, this method has penetrated the heart of philosophical development.

The growth of our intellectual life can, therefore, occur in three different directions: (1) in a sort of continuous homogeneous extension; (2) in a leaping break which goes beyond the many to reach unity, to reach its source; and (3) in an increasingly tense opposition which seeks to give rise to something new, like a spark emerging from the violence of a shock.

These three directions are qualitatively very different, and they enrich our mind in very different ways: a quantitative enrichment in the order of extension; a qualitative enrichment of 'penetration,' of discovery of what is primary; and a more artistic enrichment which claims to attain a superior harmony in a synthesis; the synthesis is something produced by an artistic intellect.

These are three dimensions of the becoming of our intellect: a dimension of extension (our intellect seeks to render explicit the riches it possesses); a dimension of penetration (our intellect seeks to dig ever deeper); and a dimension of artistic efficiency (our intellect is capable of building itself up, developing itself).

These three becomings of the intellect indeed have, like every becoming, a starting point and a term (*terminus*). The term is what determines the becoming, what gives it its meaning. The first of these becomings is ordered to a consequence, a fruit, a conclusion; the second is ordered to the discovery of what is prior, a principle, a cause; and the third is ordered to a synthesis, a work.

The perfect becoming of the mind is realized in reflection, in a 'retreat' of the mind into itself. We enter into a sort of 'rumination' of the mind, into meditation. But the mind can be tempted by such withdrawal to discover its deepest aspect, 'itself.' This is an example of the living being rejoicing in its autonomy, claiming to find its end inside itself.

Although it claims to find its end in itself, this vital becoming is perhaps not what is most perfect in the life of the intellect. Our intellect is capable of going beyond itself and of discovering an*other*. The intellect is capable of discovering what is not itself, what brings it some fresh air and permits it to open itself, to let itself be determined and find its end in something or someone whom it does not have in itself.

The most characteristic intellectual operation is not the becoming of the mind (although this is the most manifest) but what we call a judgment. It is easy to recognize that reasoning, like becoming, is not first: it is always relative to, and presupposes, something else. Of course, we can ignore and forget this fact, but if we want to be perfectly lucid, we are obliged to recognize it. Can we not say that all reasoning presupposes a judgment, just as all becoming presupposes being? Can we not say that all reasoning is brought to completion in a judgment, just as all becoming ends in that-which-is.

Judgment appears to be the most perfect operation of intellectual knowledge because it is both the foundation of reasoning and its end. What characterizes judgment is its perfect awareness, its perfect consciousness. Indeed, what is proper to our judgments is that they possess self-lucidity. I am conscious of thinking about someone, or even of reflecting upon and judging the very quality of my judgments: Are they accurate? Are they erroneous? This lucidity comes from the fact that intellectual knowledge occurs beyond the physical world. There is no more juxtaposition but, on the contrary, perfect immanence.

This consciousness is not the principal thing in judgment, but it is, as it were, the property of judgment on the side of the knowing subject: I am conscious of reflecting. Consciousness is, so to speak, the first 'possession' of the knowing subject. One could add that, as reasoning requires reflection in order to be perfectly itself, so judgment demands consciousness in order to be perfectly itself. This consciousness, in fact, has different degrees of intensity, from the clear consciousness of certain intuitions to the more opaque and more difficult to discern consciousness of certain practical judgments.

If consciousness is only a property of judgment we must not stop at it, but, through consciousness, discover what judgment is in itself. Judgment is the act of intellectual knowledge *par excellence*, for it allows us to affirm or deny that a particular reality exists. Judgment also allows us to grasp philosophical principles such as 'happiness is man's end.' It allows us to state scientific laws. It allows us to affirm scientific conclusions. All of these are judgments, but of different types. Our judgments occur in great diversity, from the judgment of existence – 'this is,' 'this is not' – to the judgment stating the conclusion of reasoning, such as, 'the passion of anger is the most violent passion.'

Nevertheless, diverse as they may be, all these judgments involve a composition or division which results from our affirming or denying. It is within ourselves, in our inmost intellectual life, that the composition 'this is' or the division 'this is not' occurs; 'Peter walks' or 'Peter does not walk.' The composition or the division, which occurs at the intentional level, has meaning. It expresses something that exists, or can exist, in reality. This something that exists or can exist is what determines and specifies this vital operation of knowledge. A living being endowed with spiritual life affirms and denies through such composition and division. In affirming, he commits himself; he adheres to what he says. In denying, he also commits himself, but in reverse: he refuses to adhere. This is what characterizes the particular mode of this vital operation: judgment occurs in commitment (engagement) regarding reality or in a suspension of commitment.

The suspension of judgment can lead to an intellectual dilettantism which in turn leads to 'cerebralization,' as psychologists would say; that is to say, an intellectual life that no longer has any real content, that is satisfied with play, the consideration of possibles (possibilities). The intellect is not primarily made for this; in fact, it is a 'distraction' with respect to the true life of the intellect. The intellect is made for adherence, for commitment to reality, a reality that it recognizes and seeks to know further.

Thanks to adherence or a refusal to adhere, our intellect affirms or denies; it fully affirms in declaring 'this is true,' and it fully denies in declaring 'this is false.' When the intellect affirms 'this is true,' it commits itself fully and bears the responsibility. And it recognizes that what it says, what it states, conforms to reality, to life. The intellect recognizes that it is not inventing or dreaming, letting itself be taken up by the imagination. It recognizes that it is no longer in the realm of possibilities, but attains to that which exists, to 'that-which-*is*'.

It may very well happen that our intellect lose its 'virility' and become unable to assert that what it states is true. The human intellect may even come to say that it is unable, by itself, to do so. At that moment the intellect no longer affirms 'that-which-is,' but affirms its own incapacity; it affirms something while claiming that it cannot affirm anything as true. The intellect then places itself in an unacceptable position, for its affirmation is no longer an affirmation. It withdraws into a realm of pure hypotheses.

When the intellect asserts 'this is true,' it acknowledges both its nobility and its dependence. The intellect is capable of grasping this or that present reality, this or that principle, and knowing that what it grasps is true — that is, conformable to 'that-which-is.' Such is the nobility of an intellect capable of knowing reality as it is, in its most profound aspect. But the intellect can only know a reality if it accepts being dependent upon and completely relative to it. The intellect must accept receiving its proper determination from reality. Indeed, the intellect recognizes that it grasps 'that-which-is' because what it grasps comes from 'that-which-is'. The intellect has not made reality – except when the reality is a work of art (the intellect can then judge truth in reverse, because it is source of the reality – which is new). Moreover, the intellect is capable of discerning and grasping its own twofold (speculative and practical) orientation, as we have already said. What is important to point out here is that truth – the perfection of the intellect – can be realized in various ways. We shall return to this point in critical reflection.

We must also understand that judgment – once again, the perfect operation realized in composition or division – is not simple but complex. Consequently, it cannot be an elementary operation; it presupposes another in that it includes another. It includes an operation of apprehension, of grasping. Because of our consciousness of the judgment, we can discover this. The judgment whereby one affirms 'this is,' involves a certain grasp of the 'this' prior to the simple (the simplest) affirmation itself ('this is'). Otherwise the affirmation would be of something unknown. However indistinct, one must have a grasp of the 'this' in its determination. Such indistinct or obscure under-standing begs for precision, for we seek clarity. One cannot be content with a vague vision of reality. We seek more precise knowledge; we wish to define. Was this not Socrates' desire? His method of irony revealed that, most of the time, people do not understand the deep meaning of what they say. People only know names and stop at them as if they were things, instead of considering them to be signs (what the Greeks called *symbola*) of what we conceive of reality. In so doing people forget what the intellect is made for. Our intellect, in its primary appetite, seeks to know what reality is. Consequently, the intellect seeks to know the generic aspect of a reality, what it has in common with others, so that it can then discover its proper and specific aspect, what distinguishes it from others.

This primary fundamental knowledge has something particular. The mode of its assimilation is 'intentional.' In grasping what a reality is, we 'become' the reality – not *really* but *intentionally*. We become the reality in so far as the 'form' or proper determination of the reality is present to our thought, not as it exists in the reality but in another way, abstracted from the individual, material details present in the imag-inative representation – details which are set aside as soon as we try to grasp the essential meaning of the reality. Here lies the difference between representing an existent reality – for example, such-and-such a dog – and grasping its proper meaning – *what* a dog *is*. The grasp of the intellect as it seeks to define what the reality is, to apprehend its deep meaning, lies at this level. The form, present in an abstract way to our thinking, our thought, 'exists' in it with an intentional mode. In other words, the form is present, yet totally relative to the reality from which it comes. The form is there for the reality, in lieu of it, allowing our intellect to apprehend the reality and intentionally 'become' the reality. The reality is not modified by my thinking it; rather, the reality determines my knowledge, specifies it, renders it 'signifying.' To be more precise: the reality, in and through its form, is the proper object of this intellectual grasp, this elementary operation of my intellect. We can say that the form, inasmuch as it is in my intellect and determining it, is an 'intentional' form, that is, completely relative to another and taking its place. From a critical viewpoint, we can specify that this grasp of the intellect has as an immanent fruit: a 'concept,' the meaning of which is expressed through the words we use to speak and communicate our thoughts to others. Words, therefore, are 'symbols,' conventional signs of our concepts. They are not the proper 'place' of meaning. The place of meaning is our concepts.

It is important to order and structure these three characteristic operations of our intellectual knowledge, our life at the level of the mind. In its most elementary operation – the grasp of realities – life, at the level of the mind, possesses the most fundamental vital mode, that of assimilation. The analogy between nutrition and respiration (fundamental acts of the vegetative life) and apprehension (the fundamental act of the life of the mind) is easy to establish; but we must respect the analogy, in other words, the absolute diversity of these two vital operations. Otherwise we shall not avoid the critique of Sartre with respect to a 'vegetative' conception of intellectual knowledge.[9] It is assimilation in both cases, but at two totally different levels. They are, therefore, completely different assimilations. If we respect the analogy, we can say that aliment, or food, is to the vegetative life what the object is to our life of thought; otherwise it leads to great confusion. Food does not determine assimilation in vegetative life; it is only the assimilable matter. The vital power of vegetative life determines the assimilation; and this vital power varies among living beings. In the life of the mind, on the contrary, the *object*, precisely speaking (that is, not the existent reality in its individuality but that which essentially determines the

9 Jean-Paul Sartre, *Situations*, I.

reality, its form[10]), specifies and determines my grasp, my thought. The vital power capable of knowing at the level of the spirit – the intellect (what the Greeks called νουσ, *nous*) – is a receptive power as regards determination, or form, although it is in act (active) as regards vital exercise.

The (perfect) operation of judgment has a mode of adherence and engagement which allows it to confront existent reality and distinguish itself from it, recognizing the anteriority of the latter and itself as true in so far as it conforms to reality.

Finally, the operation of reasoning, which is the becoming of our intellectual life, stems from what we can call 'reason,' our rational intellect. The proper mode of intellectual becoming is not assimilation or adherence, but a certain vital growth: there is, as it were, progress and development from within. This becoming is a sort of fruitfulness in so far as its conclusion is a 'fruit.' In this sense we can say that, with respect to such becoming, reason is a vital source: a source of progress, and widening its field of knowledge and discoveries. Reason does not receive a new specification from without; from its own riches, it draws out (makes explicit) new knowledge. That is why reason is the operation in which the vital aspect of the intellect – the *se-movere* and fruitfulness – is most manifest. The intellect then discovers something new; it discovers it either from prior knowledge or from its own exercise.

It is easy to see that if we reduce the life of the intellect to this becoming we are in the presence of dialectical idealism. If we reduce the life of the intellect to its first grasp, we are in the presence of ideological idealism: the primacy of idea over existent reality. In reality, only the recognition of the operation of judgment as the most perfect intellectual operation allows us to safeguard realism. With this recognition we affirm the primacy of existent reality over our intellectual life – while recognizing that our intellect, in its activity of primary apprehension, assimilates what is immediately intelligible in the existent reality; at this elementary level of the intellectual life there is indeed a sort of formal (intentional) unity between the object and the intellect.

Given the great diversity in the exercise of these three operations, and also given the great flexibility of each of these operations, we could ask if all of them really arise from the same vital spiritual power.

10 Aristotle invented an expression for this – *to ti en einai* – translated into Latin as *quod quid erat esse* and then simplified as *quidditas* (quiddity). We must rediscover the meaning of the Greek expression: *that which is* essential in the fact of existing. This is what is immediately intelligible.

All of them have the same *radical* source of life, the spiritual soul, the same soul that informs our body. Yet we can further specify that all have the same proper, *immediate* source: the intellect, the *nous*; for, although diverse in their exercise, these various operations have something in common beyond their determination and proper specification. This 'something' in common is that-which-is. Apprehension is indeed specified by form; judgment affirms the very existence of that-which-is, as existence; and the becoming of our intellect is specified by relation. Form, the act of being, and relation are indeed three modes of 'that-which-is.' That-which-is is present in these three modes; it alone unifies them and alone can unify them. We then understand the meaning of an affirmation from Avicenna, taken up and given new meaning by Thomas Aquinas: *primo in intellectu cadit ens*: that which 'falls' first into the intellect is that-which-is, being. It is indeed the intellect as a spiritual power of knowledge that progressively, successively, penetrates more deeply into that-which-is in order to know it and grasp all its intelligibility. The intellect first grasps that-which-is by assimilating what it can assimilate (its form); it then knows that-which-is by adhering to it, letting itself be measured by it; lastly, it uses relation to understand better the unity between form and the act of being, *esse* – not to synthesize them but to grasp their unity while respecting their distinction.

Note, moreover, the distinction that Thomas Aquinas, following Aristotle, makes between *intellectus* and *ratio*.[11] For him, they are two completely different functions of the same power of knowledge: judgment and apprehension (*intellectus*), and reasoning (*ratio*).

WILL

Our life at the spiritual level involves a volitional affective development concurrent with the development of knowledge: our acts of love regarding a spiritual good, our acts of intention regarding an end, in other words, everything analyzed in ethics. These acts are volitional and arise from a spiritual appetite, an affective power capable of loving a spiritual good and mobilizing our energies to acquire it. This power is what we call the will. It primarily concerns all that is good in so far as it is good; yet it can only stop at and find its end in a *spiritual* good, that is, a person. This is clear as soon as we analyze the most characteristic acts of the spiritual appetite. Think of friendship which we have already analyzed. The most characteristic act of our spiritual appetite is an act

11 *Summa Theologica*, Ia, Q79 art 8.

of love. This act is the deepest, most radical awakening of our will. Our will is made for loving, for connecting with its spiritual good, that which is capable of perfecting the spiritual living being and bringing it to completion. The will is properly the spiritual appetite of a living being and is the affective power of the human person. By the will, the person himself loves, that is, lets himself be attracted to a spiritual good, to another person capable of perfecting him and being his end. It is paramount to understand that our will is first a capacity for spiritual, personal love, and not first a power for efficacy, or efficiency, as Descartes asserts. By the will, a person is not first capable of dominating, commanding, giving orders, saying 'do this,' but of loving, accepting the immediate influence of a spiritual good, letting himself be attracted to it, and responding by giving himself and affectively and spiritually welcoming it. Behold the 'spiritual heart,' which is none other than the will in its most profound aspect. The 'spiritual heart,' the will, is first of all a power for receptivity with respect to a spiritual good; but in order for the good to attract, it must be known by the intellect as a spiritual good – not in an abstract, universal way, but in a concrete way, in its proper existence. The good, in what it is, indeed implies an act of being, of existing (an ideal good is not, properly speaking, a good; and a sensible good, known as a sensible good, is not attained in its existence but only in its appearance, its phenomenon; and thus not really as a good). A good must be reached in a judgment of existence. This judgment, which unveils the existence of the spiritual good, allows it to unveil itself as a good, i.e., to awaken love in the inmost depths of the will; and from this there is new, affective knowledge of a good, for I know it from within as my good. It is the existent good itself which determines my love and is its end. The knowledge of the intellect permits an indispensable contact, but it is not what determines my spiritual appetite, my will. We have already seen this at the levels of friendship and passion; we are pointing it out here at the level of the birth of the spiritual first love.

This spiritual first love is not, in and of itself, conscious; it is only conscious in friendship, in intention and choice.[12] Yet a philosopher discovers the existence of this spiritual first love as fundamental to the development of our volitional operations. This first love is the starting point of our spiritual affective life. Moreover, it does not stop growing; for at the spiritual level we have in us an infinite capacity for loving a spiritual good. There are no limits – except the necessities of practical daily life – to the deep *élan* of our spiritual heart. This underground

12 See above, p. 26 and following.

source within us begs to blossom, to flow, to love the one who is our good, whom we have profoundly discovered as our good and who attracts us so radically – we could say wildly – beyond all conditioning. This is what is proper to love.

If we analyze this spiritual love, we discover in it the two main aspects of love, already mentioned in connection with love-passion. It is an ecstatic *élan* or movement of the heart towards the loved good, i.e., the person who is loved. And it is a gift of self, of that which is most profound, most intimate, and most alive in us, but with an intentional, not a substantial, mode. Our living-being, at its most radical and substantial level, cannot become spiritual love, a gift to another. In itself, our living-being is not our love, although it is the radical source of this love. We can further point out that, although the soul is the substantial principle of being in us, the principle of autonomy, it is not substantially our ecstatic love towards another. Although the soul immediately structures the living being in itself, it is only mediately the source of spiritual love; nevertheless, the soul allows the spiritual living being to love and give himself. That is why spiritual love allows us to discover what is most radical in our soul: radically it is love, a capacity to give. This shows how easy it is to confuse being and love at the level of our spiritual life.

While spiritual love is first an ecstatic *élan*, it is also a welcoming of the other, a welcoming of the loved good. It gives us a new receptivity to the other – again, according to an intentional mode. This explains how, with regard to spiritual love, this fundamental love calls for a blossoming into reciprocal love, into friendship, in order to be fully itself. For the loved good can only be welcomed if he gives himself, and he can only welcome us if he loves us. Love for the known spiritual good – which is the proper fruit of the good in us – requires that the spiritual good himself be transformed into spiritual love for the one who loves him, in order to allow love to be perfect, fully itself.

Although the first act of the will is indeed that of loving, this is not the only act of the will. Love is transformed into a 'decision' and, from that moment onward, the will becomes the source of efficiency. A decision requires a certain efficiency if it is to be true. The ultimate decision is the decision regarding execution (which the decision orders). At that moment, the will 'yields' to the intellect and we have an effacement of love, a sort of death of love, so that the final decision (that of the commandment) may be perfectly realized. This decision is the work of the intellect within a will of intention and choice. It is true that only the intellect can order efficiency if it is to be fully itself; yet its profound source remains the will. Love, in and of itself, calls for fruitfulness; yet the will of intention, using the intellect with a view to more immediate efficiency, can very easily become the rival of love. Normally, there should be no rivalry, but rather cooperation, because fruitfulness and efficiency are at two different levels. Fruitfulness involves a communication of life; efficiency implies the domination and transformation of matter or the use of different faculties. Nevertheless, given that our capital of life is limited, there is often a sort of rivalry between fruitfulness and efficiency. Hence we so easily oppose warm-hearted persons and efficient persons. In the latter, intellect prevails over spiritual love, which always risks being stifled. The prevalence of efficacy is the great tragedy of a technical civilization.

There is yet another voluntary act which is particularly significant: that of choice. Choice is a spiritual act where cooperation between the intellect and spiritual love is perfect. Choice is truly the operation of these two powers in order to realize a spiritual act which remains an act of love; indeed, in choosing we declare to the one whom we choose that we love him. But this act also involves an order, a preference, a judgment of estimation, and thus involves the intellect. The latter must then be completely ordered to love in order to allow it to be a love of predilection. This is most obvious when choosing a friend, yet it is true of every choice.

It is curious to find here again the two modes of the free voluntary act already noted with respect to artistic and ethical activity. Indeed, there is one mode of the free voluntary act at the level of exercise and efficacy, and another at the level of choice, for we can exercise or fail to exercise a particular vital activity and we can choose a particular friend, or a particular means in order to acquire what we desire. In the first mode of free act, the intellect seems to dominate; in the second, spiritual love seems to dominate. What is certain is that a free act presupposes both an understanding of the relationship between an end-good (considered as an absolute) and a means-good (considered as relative), and the loving will of this end-good and means-good in conformity or otherwise with the loved end. The loved end is ultimately either a friend, or God the Creator about whom religious traditions speak, or even ourselves, the source of these operations whom, with selfish love, we consider as best. We are indeed capable of considering ourselves as the end of our human activities and relativizing in our favor the other goods we choose in order to exalt ourselves. This freedom is doubtless morally deficient, yet it exists, and it involves the love of a good considered as an end and a judgment ordering various means towards the exaltation of this end.

It would be interesting to specify how our will can dominate the perfect living being that we are, i.e., to specify the various ways in which this power of our will commands the operations of our vegetative, sensitive, and intellectual life. How and to what extent can the will take charge of the complexity of man, this perfect living being?

Our will does not have direct power over the operation of our vegetative life. It only has an indirect power of application, of exercise. I can voluntarily apply myself to breathing and to eating; yet I cannot have direct control over my digestion and sleep. Doubtless, by means of certain muscular movements, or gymnastics, I can relax (or, on the contrary, strain myself), which might help my digestion, which might help me to sleep. I can avoid certain occasions where I know my sexual instinct will be excited and risk being vehemently aroused. Yet there are cases where this power over oneself is so restricted as to have no mastery whatsoever over the exercise of the instincts. In imminent danger of death, my voluntary power can apparently be annihilated, e.g., I can voluntarily no longer exercise breathing, and death ensues.

In our sensitive life, our will can act by having us, for example, to look, touch or, on the contrary, close our eyes ... Here the will can immediately dominate the exercise of these external powers: it is free to use and exercise (but not to choose, for the specification of our external senses does not depend upon us). With respect to our imagination and passions, our will no longer has the direct, immediate power to stop or suspend imaginative or passional development. It has an indirect, 'political,' power: if we are very attentive and very focused on something, we are necessarily less attentive to other occupations; these then diminish in vitality and are thereby pacified. Consequently, applying oneself very attentively to manual labor – or intellectual labor, at least for some – pacifies the agitation of the imagination and the passions.

Our will can have direct power over the execution of our movements and our behavior. We can straighten ourselves, stand, lie down, walk, run as we wish. Here again there is a freedom of exercise, but also a certain degree of freedom of choice. Everything depends upon the flexibility of our body, our muscles, and their resistance. There is a threshold, however, beyond which we cannot pass; this varies with age; and certain maladies – paralysis, for example – can clearly suppress this *dominium* of the will.

As for our intellect, by our will we apply ourselves to reflecting, thinking, and exercising the intellect; but our will cannot render us more intelligent than we are. It can, however, enable us to acquire *habitus*, through activity, and thus increase our capacity for comprehension, for deeper and broader understanding. Yet, strictly speaking, the will does not have freedom of choice when it comes to the intellect. Such freedom is only exercised within the development of voluntary activities (and thus has a much narrower field than the freedom of exercise).

We can thus see how man's whole life is, in a certain sense, under the ascendency of his will. We can also see how the will is limited and how the will truly makes a free choice only in a relatively restricted interior field. Hence, defining man in reference to freedom lacks realism; yet doing so can be appealing and contains some measure of truth, for the freedom of exercise indirectly extends to our entire human life and envelops it.

If we analyze these various operations at the level of the life of our spirit, we discover the proper immanence of this life; we discover its true interiority. We then realize that the immanence of imaginary sensitive life remains 'peripheral' compared to the immanence of the life of the spirit, for the imagination makes us leave the true interiority of thought and spiritual love and places us in a state of distraction. A representative image does not enable us to enter into true interiority.

Having analyzed these different degrees of life, a philosopher poses the question: Does death, which divides by separating the soul from the body, free the spiritual soul from its bond with the body, as Plato and Plotinus conceived of it, or does death incur the destruction of both body and soul as a result of this division? The question arises because we have no experience of a separated soul; we only have the experience, with a corpse, of the destruction of what was a body. In other words, can the spiritual soul survive death? Can it exist after death? Can it exist separately?

The analysis of the various operations of the life of the spirit alone does not allow us to give an absolute answer. It only reveals that the operations of the intellect – which reach universal, proper principles, and necessary and universal laws – are, in their proper structure, immaterial and thus seem to indicate that their source, the spiritual soul, is likewise immaterial, beyond the becoming of the physical world, and that it possesses deep interiority. The interiority of spiritual love and thought is the proper fruit of the spiritual soul; and indeed, this interiority seems to indicate that the spiritual soul is capable of an autonomous, personal life whose limits and boundaries we cannot see. It has, as it were, a capacity for the infinite, an opening towards the infinite.

Nevertheless, we cannot affirm absolutely that our spiritual soul subsists in and by itself, separate from the body; for its vital affective and intellectual operations have an intentional mode. The universal is not a substantial reality but a 'being of reason.' That is why we cannot immediately affirm that our spiritual soul is capable of subsisting by itself after death, separate from the body. Yet we can say that the development of our spiritual life, as regards both affectivity and thought, seems to indicate and even demand it. The question is clearly stated; yet we cannot respond at the level of philosophy of the living being; only first philosophy, in its ultimate development, will allow us to respond.

8

THE FIRST STAGE OF FIRST
PHILOSOPHY (METAPHYSICS)[1]

JUDGMENT OF EXISTENCE

We cannot stop our philosophical analysis here, because the four
experiences upon which we have based our inquiry (work, friendship,
that which is moved, and that which moves itself), although irreducible, have something in common. Work is an experience belonging to
man, as is friendship. That which is moved is primarily man; and the
primary living being is also man. Man is present in these four
experiences and gives them their deep unity. And so we must ask
'What is man?' Now, we can only know man through our experience of
him. And there is a fundamental experience of ourselves that we have
not yet considered: our assertion that 'I am,' 'I exist.' Through work,
man indeed experiences that he exists. In loving a friend, man
experiences that he exists. When he is moved, man experiences that he
exists. In living, in being alive, man also experiences that he exists. If
man experiences that he exists in these different ways, he can consider
what they have in common and seek to elucidate, or make explicit,
their common foundation. He can then assert 'I exist,' 'I am,' and
recognize that he exists like the other realities around him. In the
judgment of existence in which I affirm 'I exist,' I can stress either the
'I' or the 'exist.' If I stress the 'I,' it is no longer, properly speaking, a
judgment of existence. I simply assert myself as existing; it is 'I' that I
consider above all else. I am oriented unknowingly toward Descartes'
assertion: 'I think, therefore I am.' When asserting that I think, I do
indeed grasp that I exist. But when asserting that I love, I also grasp
that I exist; and when asserting that I work, I grasp that I exist.

I can also stress the 'exist,' without suppressing the 'I,' but
relativizing it; the fact of existing is what is considered above all. The
judgment of existence then stands out. And it does not matter whether

1 We refer the reader to our work, *L'être. Recherche d'une philosophie première* (2
volumes, the second in two parts; Téqui, Paris, 1972–4).

I say 'I am' or 'this is.' The only difference is that when asserting 'this is' I call upon experience involving the external senses, especially that of touch; whereas I can say 'I exist' merely by thinking. But then the danger is that the 'I' may be too present and veil the fact of existing. That is why it is good to express a judgment of existence both ways in order not to be tempted to remain in the 'self,' and so that 'exist' might stand out in its act of being.

It is easy to see why we cannot agree with Descartes; with the *cogito*, the 'I exist' is not what is primarily experienced. It is experienced through the vital activity of thought or love. Thus, in his approach, it is either through an intentional content or through reflection upon the exercise of voluntary activity that I grasp that 'I exist'; it is by means of a mode of being that I assert that I exist. On the contrary, we must be wholly attentive to the simplest, most direct judgment of existence there is: the one that asserts 'this is' or 'I am.'

It could be objected that a judgment of existence always takes place in an experience, and thus that we assert the existence of *something*. It is always by means of a determination – 'this' – that 'is' is asserted. Whether the determination is 'this,' or an intentional form, or the very exercise of vital activity, it is always by means of a determination that existence, or existing, is reached. Would it not then be better to choose a more spiritual determination such as *cogito* (thought) rather than a physical reality?

It is correct to say (as language shows) that the judgment of existence, 'this is,' is always made through a 'this.' But in the judgment of existence, that which is first asserted is not 'this' but 'is'; the accent is placed on *is*. This is the difference between 'I think, therefore I am' and 'this is.' In the assertion 'I think, therefore I am,' thought is first considered and experienced, and then I discover the existence ('I am') it implies. However, when I assert or say 'this is,' the existent reality, grasped by my intellect (bound to my senses, to touch) is reached, is experienced. It is true that I affirm that 'such-and-such reality' exists, but it is its *existing*, its *act of being*, which is highlighted.

That is why we must underscore the difference between these two affirmations: 'I think, therefore I am' (or 'I love, therefore I am') and 'this is.' In the former, it is by means of a mode of that-which-is – however noble it may be ('I think') – that I discover existing; whereas in the latter, the existing as act of being is reached immediately. It is not reached, of course, in all purity (otherwise we would have an intuition of being). It is reached in the 'this,' in such-and-such reality; but it is reached directly and explicitly. Thus it is no longer reached by a form, or a manner of existing, but through and beyond such-and-such determination (without the determination being separated from it). It is grasped directly and explicitly. The intellect is capable of fully highlighting existence: 'this *is*.'

Here we have, as it were, a new, fundamental experience – we might say, a meta-experience – implicitly present in all the others, yet which demands to be considered in itself. A philosopher does not have the right to neglect it, claiming that it is of no interest. That would be an a priori, the most terrible of all, for it concerns what is most fundamental and primary. A philosopher must be attentive to this primary experience. And as soon as he is attentive to it, he wonders why it is so often neglected and so easily forgotten, why determinations, forms, and this or that reality grab attention, while that which *is* is forgotten precisely in so far as it is.[2] Where does this forgetfulness come from? How is it that man remains so superficial? It is due to the conditioning of his human life and, more precisely, the conditioning of the life of his mind, his intellect. With sensations and imagination the intellect awakens. Sensations have to do with qualities or forms and the imagination with the realm of quantity. The intellect, awakening with and after the senses and the imagination, has great difficulty in truly being itself. Very often it lingers in lazy continuity with imaginative sensitive knowledge and does not emerge beyond it. The intellect is, as it were, inhibited, trapped in initial sensitive knowledge, not going beyond the realm of forms, unable to discover its proper domain, that for which it is primarily made. The intellect remains unable to discover that-which-is in so far as it is.

Surprised that such an experience can be so readily forgotten, the philosopher himself does not want to forget it; he dwells upon it. This experience arouses profound admiration: what he sees in the universe, what exists around him, those whom he loves, all *are*, all *exist*. This is what is common to all and, at the same time, what is most proper to

2 Heidegger denounced the forgetting of being in Western philosophy since Parmenides. Would it not be more exact to say that, in reality, the judgment of existence, 'this is,' has been forgotten since Ockham ... and that Heidegger himself forgot it? The being of which Heidegger speaks is being which appears in thought, inseparable from thought. It is not 'that-which-is.' For Heidegger, that-which-is is the limited being that we experience, *essent*, to use a term coined by Ralph Manheim in his translation of Martin Heidegger, *An Introduction to Metaphysics* (Yale University Press, 1987). Grammatically speaking, it is being in the progressive tense. Being *is* not in itself; it is thought. Heidegger remains too closely linked to Kant and Hegel and does not rediscover 'that-which-is' as being (because, according to him, it is necessary to negate that-which-is, this limited being, so that being might appear in thought). See my *Une philosophie de l'être est-elle encore possible?*, fascicule II, p. 287, and fascicule IV, pp. 87 ff. (Téqui, Paris, 1975).

each. All are, all exist (if they did not exist they would be nothing); yet
each, in what it is (in its most intimate core, so to speak) exists: it *is*.
Moreover, opposed to 'this is' is the most radical opposition: 'this is
not.' One cannot go further than 'this is not.' Before that which is not,
the intellect and the will can say nothing and want nothing. That
which is not has no form, no being, it is not intelligible, and it is not
lovable. We could conclude that it is useless and serves no purpose to
speak of what does not exist. It is useful, given the conditioning of our
intellect (an intellect which does not have an intuition of being). The
radical opposition 'this is not' admirably manifests the primacy of 'that-
which-is' and, from this viewpoint, is not negligible. Shadow helps us
grasp the light! Our intellect, given its weakness and the risk it runs of
dwelling in 'forms,' makes use of such an opposition to become itself, to
be wholly in the presence of that-which-is to be in the wonder of the
encounter with that-which-is. That-which-is actuates my intellect. It
truly makes it intelligent in act. In asserting 'this is' my intellect
thinks perfectly. It awakens to its proper life as intellect, because from
'this is,' the intellect asks, What is being? What is non-being? What is
this opposition of which the intellect is the source and which is so
radical? Why is the intellect capable of asserting non-being? These are
the main questions through which we enter this new realm, which is
both familiar and strange, always near and always transcendent: the
realm of being. Indeed, this questioning, which arises from the most
radical experience (intellect bound to touch) in the judgment of
existence, 'this is,' makes us immediately discover both our greatest
closeness to that-which-is and our separation from an existent other. I
discover that-which-is as that which exists, as I myself exist. There is no
longer a distinction between object and knowing subject, for both
exist. In so far as they are, they are one. I also discover that that-which-
is is not me; it is the other, and it will never be me, precisely in so far as
it *is*. The question 'what is being?' thereby manifests the deepest
appetite of our intellect, which cannot stop at forms or the exercise of
our activities, but wants to attain to what is ultimate in existent
reality.

It is important to note that in this question the intellect attains *being*
for the first time. In the judgment of existence, it asserts 'that which *is*';
in questioning it specifies 'what is being?' The passage from 'that
which is' to 'being' is very significant. In questioning that-which-is –
grasped in a judgment of existence – the intellect approaches being.
There is a difference, then, which distinguishes this position from that
of Heidegger. For him, that-which-is is limited experiential being,
essent, and *essent* does not lead to Being. On the contrary, that-which-is

must be rejected and, from Nothingness, Being appears. Heidegger affirms this because of a certain influence of Hegelian dialectic. In reality, if nothingness can manifest being, it is only beginning with a grasp of being and not the opposite (at least in a realistic perspective). In the dialectical perspective of idealism, the opposite can be held, because negation and affirmation are correlative and summon each other. In such a perspective, it can be asserted that being must appear out of nothingness. Moreover, that-which-is is concretely in the act of being, it is. Being, however, is a certain formalization. Being *per se* does not exist. That is why, if metaphysical research begins with being, there is always a risk of idealizing it. In fact, inquiry would then begin with an *idea* of being. Heidegger did not want this, and strongly opposed it. Consequently, he began with nothingness, because for him that-which-is is only grasped as *essent*. However, the question is: is beginning with nothingness still not beginning with something the intellect has constructed, a 'being of reason' still further from reality than the idea of being? Heidegger's intention is undoubtedly good, but it remains too dependent upon Hegelian dialectic. In order to respond to his intention, we must go further in realism and rediscover the strength of the judgment of existence, this *is*.

SUBSTANCE ('OUSIA')

In order to answer the question 'What is being?,' we must return to our experience of that-which-is and seek to grasp what primarily is, in that-which-is. We must seek to grasp that-which-is in an absolute fashion. We must seek the core of its being. As already shown, the question 'What is this?' seeks the principle and cause in the order of determination. In our present perspective, that of questioning being, the question 'What is it?' seeks the principle and cause in the order of determination of that-which-is considered from the viewpoint of being, considered as being. This principle and cause is what Aristotle called *ousia* (a word awkwardly translated into Latin as *substantia*, substance). Plato had already recognized *ousia* as that which is beyond becoming (what the Greeks called *genesis*), as that which remains.[3]

In the history of Western philosophy, 'substance' has taken on several meanings: subject, form, soul, etc. As post-Hegelian philosophy

3 Cf. the etymology given by Plato for the word *ousia* in the *Cratylus* (401 c–e): he links it to Hestia, the goddess who 'dwells in the house of the gods, all alone' (*Phaedrus* 247a).

has developed, substance has been progressively rejected. Relation has taken its place, and being has come to be viewed as a fabric of relations. The development of the physical sciences – notably the theory of relativity – has greatly influenced this reduction of being to relation via the rejection of substance. Thus it is important today for a philosophy of being to reconsider thoroughly the question of substance in order to see if it is in fact a real question or a pseudo-question.

Given the difficulty we have in really analyzing that-which-is from the viewpoint of being – and thus of answering the question 'what is the principle and the cause, in the order of determination, of that-which-is considered from the viewpoint of being?' – we must return to the experience of the reality we know best – man – and make use of what we have already analyzed. In the end, it is always man that a philosopher seeks to know. Even if he seeks what being is, he still seeks to know man; for if he does not grasp what being is, what is most important in man will elude him: the fact that man *is*. In this metaphysical inquiry we are no longer considering man as the perfect living being but as one who exists, one who *is* amidst other realities that exist as he does.

A question arises immediately: Is not the soul, discovered through the vital operations, sufficient to assert the existence of substance? Is not the soul man's substance, that is, the principle and cause, in the order of determination, of that-which-is? At first glance, it seems that man's substance is indeed his soul, for the soul is not only the principle and cause of his life and unity, but also of his being.

If the soul is indeed substance, however, it cannot also be said that substance, i.e., principle and cause in the order of determination of that-which-is, is the soul. That would mean that everything which has no soul does not exist. Now many realities exist which do not have a soul. Let us not reduce first philosophy to anthropology or a philosophy of the living being. Heidegger was insistent on this point. Although the question of being is posed in a privileged way with respect to man, and even living beings in general, that does not mean that the philosophy of being should be reduced to anthropology or the philosophy of the living being.

Moreover, if substance is the soul, should we then consider man's body an accident? Man's body, however, is an essential part of his human being; it is not foreign to his substance. So we cannot identify the discovery of the soul with that of substance. We cannot reduce the question of being to that of living (of life). This is an ongoing temptation for philosophy which no longer goes far enough in realism. Because it begins its philosophical reflection with thought, which measures being instead of being measured by it, idealism no longer distinguishes clearly enough life from being, soul from substance. Interestingly enough, idealism often still speaks of the soul, but not of substance.

We must therefore resume our inductive course, beginning with our experiences of that-which-is, of man in so far as he is. Man appears very complex and manifold in his being. His qualities, quantity, relations, action, possibilities for action, and capacity to be acted upon, are all part of what he *is* in varying degrees, for some of these determinations (notably relations, the capacity for acting and for being acted upon) may disappear, and man continues in what he is. If, in the midst of these various transformations, man remains himself in what he is, it means that there is something more radical in him which gives him his unity of being in its most essential aspect.

We cannot deny that, within this observable multiplicity, there is a radical and fundamental unity in existent-man at the level of what he is, in what he is, beyond his becoming and multiplicity. His becoming, his multiplicity, and his unity, however, are what he is in his being in act. But what brings about the unity in this multiplicity, through sometimes anarchic transformation? There is necessarily a principle, a source at the level of what he is, which, through the multiplicity of determinations, of forms, maintains a more radical unity of being; this source is also the origin of a variety of man's essential qualities, i.e., his affective and cognitive powers at the spiritual and sensitive level. This source at the level of what he is, this principle, is called substance. It is the radical core, in the order of that-which-is, which gives autonomy to all that man is in his being. He is a distinct being with his own unity of being. In himself, man has an irreplaceable originality of being. No existent being is or can be identical to him at the level of what he is.

Only the intellect, in such an effort of comprehension, can attain to substance as principle and cause of that-which-is in the order of determination. Owing to the diversity of determinations within a unity of being, the intellect discovers in existent man a source immanent to his being, immanent to what he is. The intellect discovers a source which radiates in all that he is. Substance, as principle and cause of that-which-is, is thus beyond the distinction between soul and body, between form-nature and matter-nature. Soul and body constitute a living being who, in its being, is one. Form-nature and matter-nature constitute a mobile being which, in its existence, possesses a certain unity. It is from this unity within diversity that we must discover substance, the hidden source of that-which-is as being.

It is understandable how substance, principle in the order of being, risks being identified with what is primary in the order of intelligibility (the quiddity), life (the soul), becoming (the subject), logic (the universal), artistic activity (the form), and moral activity (the good). All of the above are primary in their respective orders. If the diversity of these orders is not respected, however, if they are not distinguished with sufficient clarity, substance risks being reduced to one of these other 'firsts.' It is here that we can judge the level of comprehension reached by a particular philosophy.

The discovery of substance allows us to grasp the first division of that-which-is considered from the viewpoint of being: the division between substance and the other determinations of being, all that is relative to substance and can only exist by substance (what have been somewhat equivocally called 'accidents'). Substance is the source of all these determinations; consequently, each of these determinations manifests something of the richness of the source — as the operations of the living being manifest something of the richness of their hidden source, the soul.

QUALITY, QUANTITY, RELATION

In order to grasp substance better, as the source of all determinations of that-which-is, we ought to analyze successively quality, quantity, relation, etc. We cannot do so adequately here, but we can underscore a few important points.

Quality is first a form, a determination which ennobles that-which-is, and gives it its proper character, its particular physiognomy. Quality determines that-which-is by allowing it to be perfect and giving it the possibility of attaining to its proper end. To determine as it ennobles, to determine as it orders towards the proper end is what is essential in a quality. Qualities are diverse. Some order more towards the end; others ennoble more the realities they determine.

The most visible and manifest qualities are those that we see. The color and light of a body are essential to its originality; they qualify it, as do the harmony of its colors, its physiognomy, and its particular style. This is particularly true regarding man's body (think of the light in his eyes which ennobles him).

There are also natural dispositions ordered to our deeper completion. There are powers capable of acting, and the capacity to be acted upon, both at the sensitive and spiritual level. Lastly, there are acquired perfections superadded to our spiritual powers of love and knowledge, as well as to our sensitive affective powers. We call these *habitus*. At the level of the will and the sensitive affective powers these are *virtues*. At the level of the intellect are intellectual *habitus*. The ultimate, final quality is the *habitus* of wisdom which enables us to contemplate.

In order to specify what quality is from the viewpoint of being, quality must be considered relative to substance. What does it add to substance? Quality allows substance – the principle of autonomy in the order of being – to go beyond the solitude of its autonomy by orienting itself towards its end. In this sense, we can say that it is the 'disposition' of substance.

Quantity, from the viewpoint of being, is also a determination of that-which-is. However, it implies potentiality – not radical, but secondary potentiality: that of the divisible. It is a certain 'divisible form' which, because it is divisible, calls for something capable of actuating it: measurement. That which is divisible is essentially measurable, and in measuring it, it is actuated and known. A quantified reality cannot otherwise be known, for by itself it is not immediately sensible (it is not a 'proper sensible'); it remains in potency and, as such, is not immediately intelligible.

There are different modes of this divisible form. We say that a man has a particular height or a particular weight. We can also count his body parts; we can consider his being alone or amidst others. As soon as there is quantity, one can divide and add. These different modes of quantity can be reduced to two main ones: magnitude and number. Regarding magnitude, we speak of 'continuous' quantity. It involves parts or dimensions and concerns line, surface, and volume. The measure of continuous quantity is (a) point. The other mode of quantity, number, does not involve parts or dimensions. Regarding number we speak of 'discrete' quantity. Its measure is (a) unit. Continuous quantity is more fundamental, while discrete quantity is more abstract because it is beyond situation, parts and dimensions.

To understand better these two modes of quantity, it suffices to compare their respective measures: point and unit. We immediately see that one is more concrete and the other more formal, for point implies unit; it is something indivisible (in a continuum). Unit, however, does not imply point; it is only indivisible in number. One cannot divide a unit; but one can add another unit to it. A unit is thus indivisible, yet an indivisible to which one can add and which can be added to another. It is not an absolute indivisible.

Quantity allows the physical world to be a continuum with parts capable of being divided and measured. It allows living beings to expand and grow, to increase and decrease. Through quantity man is part of the universe; he is capable of being subtracted from the other parts and of being added to them. Through quantity he 'numbers' among the other parts of the universe and among other men.

Relative to being, quantity is what allows the indivisibility of substance to be measured. Thus it is the measure of substance.

Relation is what is most 'feeble' as regards being, as Aristotle used to say. It plays a very important role, of course, from a psychological viewpoint, for it manifests man's influence upon his milieu, upon his fellow men. Are not numerous and important relations often what is essential for man? Can we not thereby judge importance, influence, and power? Yet relation remains very difficult to grasp from the viewpoint of that-which-is. That is why we must first recognize relation as a true mode of that which is, i.e., not only something exterior which affects existent reality from without. For example, friendship is a real relation between two human persons; it really determines them. If one of the friends disappears and, because of this, the friendship in its concrete realism disappears, the other friend is in no way modified in his proper qualities nor in his quantity. And yet he has lost the friendship; he has lost the presence of his friend. We must recognize that relation is something real, although in a way different from quality. Quality directly ennobles the one whom it affects, whereas relation makes us first consider another; it projects us towards this other. Relation is turned *towards* the other (*pros* in Greek) before being turned towards the one who possesses it, for relation is all eyes towards the other before determining the person whom it affects.

In analyzing relation we must specify that, unlike the other secondary determinations of being, it can only be exercised between two distinct existent realities which it unites or opposes. The correlative terms which exercise a particular relation always affect at least two people, and these terms cannot be separated. They summon each other, in either uniting or opposing themselves. While substance gives that-which-is its autonomy, relation, by means of its correlative terms, makes it come out of its solitude and renders it 'interdependent' (brings about 'solidarity') with another whom it can no longer do without.

As to real relations, the two correlative terms imply a foundation that roots them in an existent reality. This foundation is either a quality (when it is a relation of similitude or dissimilitude, e.g., Peter and Paul are alike in their courage), or a quantity (a relation of equality: Peter and Paul are equal; they have the same height, the same weight . . .), or an action or passion (for example, the relation between a master and a disciple: one acts, the other is acted upon). The foundation enables us to specify the proper character of a particular relation. The foundation allows us to determine the proper character, whereas the correlative terms are at the level of the exercise of the relation; they express its existential character.

Because of its feeble character, relation is outside the order of perfection. Its foundation is what qualifies. In itself, in its proper exercise, it is neither good nor bad. Can we say then that relation is neutral? Here we touch on its character, different from that of quality. Quality refuses neutrality, for it is either ordered to a good or opposed to this order. Relation does not express 'order to a good.' In a world which has lost the sense of purpose, or end, relation reigns; relations are multiplied more and more. At a human level, socialization tends to reduce everything to a fabric of human relations. We remain in the order of exercise, of efficiency, without any reference to the good, or end.

ACT

We have asked 'What is ...?' (*ti esti* in Greek) with respect to that-which-is considered as being. We now must ask the question 'For the sake of what is that-which-is considered as being?' The questions 'What is being made of?' and 'Whence does being come?' do not allow us to discover proper causes of that-which-is considered from the viewpoint of being – which shows us that first philosophy, the philosophy of that-which-is considered as being, cannot ally itself with dialectical materialism or absolute evolutionism. Being, in what it is, in its inmost self, is beyond matter and becoming, and its proper principles cannot be at this level. The question 'What is it made of?' leads us to the discovery of matter. Now, as we have seen, being is primarily substance, the source of determinations. Consequently, being cannot radically be matter, because the latter is indetermination. And so we see the difference between a philosophical analysis of that-which-is-moved (a philosophy of nature) and of that-which-is as being (first philosophy). The primary division of mobile being, inasmuch as it is mobile, is the division between form-matter and nature-matter (nature-matter is a proper principle of the mobile being as such). The primary division of that-which-is considered as being is the division between substance and the secondary determinations (accidents). We see the error of those who claim that the distinction between matter and form is the essential distinction of realistic philosophy. It is the fundamental distinction of that-which-is-moved, but not of that-which-is considered as being. That-which-is is not immediately and directly divided into matter and form, but into substance and quality.

However, we must not oppose substance (*ousia*) and matter, but distinguish them. For we must recognize – the example of man and other living beings says it well enough – that the compound or composite realities we experience (ourselves included) exist both as substantial and material realities.

Let us distinguish substance and the way in which substance can be realized and exist. In other words, let us distinguish *what* substance is and *how* substance is. The *how* of substance is the question of individuation, of concrete and individual substance. Substance, in our physical world, implies matter with which it constitutes individual substance. In this cooperation, the matter is not prime matter *per se*, in its pure potentiality, but prime matter bound to quantity. Some have thus said that the principle of individuation is quantity implying matter – principle as what explains individuation, not principle in the full sense (that beyond which one cannot go). In this sense, quantity bound to matter cannot be principle. If an individual is distinct from others and undivided in himself, quantity, which by itself brings divisibility, allows us to speak of individuated substance. Substance in itself is indivisible. By quantified matter, it is integrated into a whole, distinguishing itself from the other parts yet remaining entirely indivisible in itself. This is how it exists in the physical world. We therefore see how first philosophy, although going beyond matter, is not opposed to it. It integrates it in its place, not as a proper constitutive principle of that-which-is considered as being, but as the constitutive co-principle of a concrete, individual being, of that-which-is-mobile.

The question concerning the origin of that-which-is as being ('Whence does being come?') cannot be answered immediately, any more than the question 'What is being made of?' That-which-is considered as being is beyond becoming and its manner of existing. What we seek to detect then are its proper principles. The efficient cause which we discover when asking 'Whence does this reality come?' is a cause which is discovered with becoming and is linked to becoming. It is a cause which remains extrinsic to reality in its proper existence. This, however, does not do away with the question of the efficient cause of that-which-is considered as being. It is the question of Creation. But, as we shall see, the question arises later in a totally different way.

Can we not say the same thing regarding final cause? Is not this causality also extrinsic? Consequently, one cannot ask the question of a final cause of that-which-is considered as being ...

To this objection we may respond that final causality is indeed extrinsic to man's activity, but that it is not bound to becoming, for it causes by means of attraction and not by means of direct contact. And precisely because it is not bound to becoming, it can be immediately integrated at the level of that-which-is considered as being. As regards being, it is an ultimate, though not external, causality. Consequently, in order to grasp perfectly that-which-is considered as being, we must unveil the end of being. As long as we have not discovered the end of being, we cannot grasp what being is *per se*. This ultimate question has often been forgotten – which is why first philosophy has often remained sterile, having lost its ultimate meaning, and turned in on itself, turning into logic or meta-psychology. When it comes to what is ultimate, losing the end, that for which it exists, is losing what it is. First philosophy is precisely the ultimate philosophy. It is fully itself only when it asks the ultimate question: 'For the sake of what is that-which-is considered as being?' and when it seeks to answer it, aware of the difficulty in responding.

It is in the light of such difficulty that we must understand the questions: 'What is the end of that-which-is as being? With a view to what is that-which-is?' It is a matter of discovering what gives that-which-is considered as being its ultimate meaning. It is a matter of specifying what that-which-is as being is for, what is ultimate in that-which-is, beyond which there is nothing. If there is nothing outside of being, positing a 'supra-being' as its end means nothing, for this 'supra-being' can be none other than being; otherwise it is nothing. Thus, we must discover in being itself, not its foundation or basic nucleus, but what is ultimate, what completes it, its proper good, what gives it its perfect development and, by this very fact, is even closer to it than its foundation: in short, its *act*, the ultimate proper principle of that-which-is.

Aristotle was the first to have posed the question, in opposition to Plato who, beyond being, posited the One and the Good. In fact, Plato was not the only one to do so. Plotinus and the whole Neoplatonic tradition did the same. The One and the Good are, as it were, a 'supra-being'; but then being is no longer present in the One and the Good. In the end, being is identified with intelligibility (with the *to ti en einai*) and is manifold. Being is form and idea, and no longer that-which-is.

For Aristotle, on the other hand, one (or oneness) is the property of being and the good is a mode of act, which in turn is the end of being. This is undoubtedly Aristotle's great discovery, a discovery quickly lost after him, recovered by Thomas Aquinas and then quickly lost again. It is a discovery each of us must make personally if our intellect is to be truly what it ought to be, if it is to blossom into wisdom, into contemplation.

Without taking up word for word the way in which Aristotle explains the discovery of act, let us nevertheless 'enroll ourselves at his school' in order to make this discovery for ourselves.

The qualities that we have studied – especially the operative *habitus*, and above all the *habitus* of wisdom – orient man towards his ultimate end, yet cannot be his ultimate end. They only allow him to attain to it with greater ease and joy. We must, therefore, go beyond the realm of quality in order to discover man's proper end, and, *a fortiori*, to discover the end of that-which-is as being. This end, because it is the cause of causes, can only be discovered by means of induction. Given its ultimate character – and consequently how difficult it is for us to discover – it requires a particularly qualitative induction, that is, an induction which uses different but parallel experiences, all with something similar.

At the level of our vegetative life we notice that we are at times awake, at times asleep. While these states are completely different, the same substantial reality experiences them successively. There is an order between them: the sleeping state is (normally!) ordered to the waking state.

At the level of our sensitive life, we have the capacity to see and we see in act: two modes of the same power. The capacity to see is obviously ordered to seeing.

At the level of the life of our spirit, we have an intellect capable of judging and attaining to truth, and we exercise it by judging and by affirming 'this is true' – again, two different modes of the same power. It is equally clear that the power of the intellect is ordered to the grasp of truth, which is its proper perfection. We can make similar remarks as regards the will. The will is capable of tending towards a good, of undergoing its attraction, and it can be united to this good, its proper end – once again, two modes of the same power, one of which is ordered to the other.

As regards our artistic life, there is an analogous observation. Someone who possesses the art of building, although capable of building, does not necessarily do so. If he builds, he realizes a work (of art). Here again are two manners of being of the same habitus (the habitus of art) and quality. Artistic capacity is ordered to the realization of a work. And with respect to a work, we can easily recognize that what is incomplete awaits completion and is ordered to this completion.

As regards our moral operations, it is easy to observe that those who possess the *habitus* of wisdom are capable of contemplating, but do not necessarily contemplate all the time. Whenever they do contemplate, they exercise their *habitus* of wisdom. Here we have the same quality realized in two different states, one of which is ordered to the other.

As regards physical reality, in the discovery of matter-nature and form-nature, we observed that one is completely ordered to the other: matter-nature is entirely ordered to form-nature, as the imperfect to the perfect.

Finally, in first philosophy, we likewise note that that-which-*is* in act – such-and-such man, for example – can *not* exist, because it is in becoming, a becoming which involves corruption (decomposition). Man's substance is an indivisible principle in the order of being; however, his manner of existing (his 'how') entails matter which renders it corruptible, and so he can not exist. His substance is thereby fragile. We again grasp that that which exists in act entails the possibility of existing, a possibility which is necessarily ordered to its act.

It is curious to note that philosophical inquiry at these various levels – those of becoming, life, moral and artistic operations, and that-which-is – can be taken up in a new way, which shows that in all the realities we experience (and in ourselves) there are, as it were, two states or poles: one wholly positive, final, and ultimate; the second, in expectation, implying a kind of privation because it is imperfect. Between these two poles, within a same reality, there is a necessary order.

Within and beyond the various realities experienced at these five levels there is something in common; there is a certain proportional (analogical) unity manifested by their order, a unity which can only be at the level of being (because that is the only common level). This 'something in common' allows our intellect to discover (thanks to the question 'For the sake of what is being?') a principle and an ultimate cause of this unity in diversity, a principle and cause which are present yet, as it were, veiled in these realities. This principle is 'being-in-act.'

What we have is a synthetic and analogical induction. In an ultimate effort, the intellect, seeking the end of that-which-is, gathers into unity the greatest diversity of states of the realities we experience.

Being-in-act is *end* in the strongest, fullest sense, for being in potency is entirely and essentially ordered to it. Being-in-act and being-in-potency are not two states of being like the two states of a person, in which he is able to see and in which he sees. Very often we project upon being our experiences at the level of life. But then we do not attain to what is proper to that-which-is considered as being. Instead of pursuing our analysis of that-which-is precisely inasmuch as it is, we restrict it to a particular manner of being – a particular form or quality. It may be interesting, but we no longer reach intellectually that-which-is as being. We limit ourselves to a descriptive aspect, to what is intentionally or affectively lived. But that-which-is, considered as such, is never experience *as it is interiorly lived* (the *vécu*). That-which-is is beyond this. It is certainly present in it, but as being, rather than as interiorly lived experience. This lived inner experience is 'of being' (it exists) – with a particular, 'intentional' mode. Thus we must go beyond; we must be careful to 'make the jump' which alone allows entry into metaphysical analysis; and here it is particularly important.

Through the experience of sight and the capacity to see, a completed work and its incompleteness, etc., at the level of being with a judgment of existence, we must grasp the division: being-in-act and being-in-potency. As we have said, they are not two states of being (for then we would remain in a sort of becoming of being, an evolution of being). It is being attained to as end-act (that for which that-which-is, is) and being attained to as potency (i.e., what, in that-which-is, is ordered to the other, to act). It is an ultimate division in being. It is indeed in a division (which entails a separation) that we grasp being-in-act. We have no intuition of it. Being-in-act never directly presents itself to us as pure being-in-act. What we experience and attain to in a judgment of existence is surely an act of being – but in and through 'this.' What it is is grasped, yet in and through a 'gangue', i.e., a particular manner of being which is not itself being-in-act. We must detect or unveil the act of being and for this we must divide or separate it from what is not it: being-in-potency. This division thus renders explicit being-in-act – the ultimate perfection and end of being – and being-in-potency – as it were, a sort of expectant being, wholly tending towards being-in-act, its end.

This is the second division of being which, as we can readily see, is completely different from the first (substance-quality). Being-in-act can be realized according to various modes at the level of substance and at the level of vital operations. Man's contemplation is not his substance. His contemplation is an immanent activity which qualifies and ennobles him. His contemplation is his *act*. It is even his ultimate act. We see thereby that the division 'being-in-act' and 'being-in-potency' is not at the same level as that of substance and the relative determinations. This division is ultimate. It goes further, encompassing the previous one which it presupposes and does not destroy. Here we grasp what analogical knowledge of being is: we have various perspectives on that-which-is considered as being, each of which is irreducible to the others, and yet all of which view that-which-is as being. We do not have a single intuitive perspective on being, but two: substance-being and act-being, and to these two views are added two relative, secondary views, views which grasp quality-being, relation-being, and potency-being.

Being grasped as act is end-being; it is ultimate principle-being. It is not form, the determination of that-which-is (substance, the source of all the determinations). Neither is it the exercise of a vital operation, however perfect this operation might be. It is being in its ultimate aspect. It is being that is perfectly being, to which nothing can be added.

Being-in-act is so ultimate that we do not have a quidditative grasp of it (we do not grasp the 'reason,' the *ratio*, of act) nor do we grasp it in itself and for itself in a judgment of existence of that-which-is, of what is directly given to us in experience. In adhering to that-which-is we grasp an act of being in its existential realization. What we grasp is a reality that exists, not being-in-act. We attain an act of being, not separated, however, from the particular mode in which it exists. Only at the end of an induction does our intellect grasp being-in-act. It grasps it in a judgment which is no longer a judgment of existence but a perfect judgment. This judgment is the ultimate operation of our intellect when it desires to penetrate that-which-is in its ultimate aspect, i.e., its act of being in its purity and limpidity as being-in-act. This being-in-act is grasped in an analogical manner, in such a way that we can only express it perfectly by opposing it to being-in-potency. We do grasp it in itself and by itself, independently of being-in-potency and prior to it. That is why we say being-in-potency is entirely relative to it. But we can only perfectly express being-in-act by separating it from being-in-potency, even opposing it, for 'saying' it perfectly in itself would require a quidditative grasp.

Being-in-act is prior to being-in-potency in different ways. It is prior in the order of perfection. This is evident because act is the *end* of being and thus the perfection of that-which-is; whereas being-in-potency is totally relative and so second to being-in-act.

Being-in-act is also prior to being-in-potency in terms of intelligibility and knowledge. It is prior in that the intellect can attain to being-in-potency only relative to being-in-act, whereas being-in-act is grasped by itself – although, once again, we can only perfectly 'say' it by opposing it to being-in-potency.

In the order of time, in the genetic order, being-in-potency is prior to being-in-act in the same individual – otherwise there would be no individual becoming or growth; for once being has reached a state of perfection – once it is fully in act – it rests and has no more becoming. But such is not the case when we consider becoming at the level of species. Here, that which is perfect is first.

Given the difficulty in grasping being-in-act and being-in-potency, we must consider their different modes. They help us to grasp better the depth of this division and its original character; we could say that as the secondary determinations of being help us to grasp substance, the source of these determinations, so the different modes of being-in-act help us to understand (although in a different way) being-in-act in all its limpidity.

The first mode of being-in-act is that of *existing*, existence, *esse*; this mode is at the level of what exists in a substantial way. Yet because of this, we must not think that substance in the precise sense – as principle and cause of that-which-is in the order of determination – is in potency with respect to *esse*. Every principle in the order of being is a certain absolute, is primary. Thus substance is not in potency with respect to being-in-act. Yet we say that *esse*, as the primary mode of being-in-act, being-in-act in the strongest sense, actuates the primary mode of being-in-potency, i.e., substantial, radical potentiality. Is not the latter the essence of existent reality? Essence, precisely speaking, cannot *be* by itself. Essence is, as it were, a capacity to be. It implies a particular determination, but this determination does not exist in and by itself. It remains in potency. It only exists thanks to a particular act of being. Moreover, even if the essence has a certain intelligibility, we can only grasp this intelligibility from the reality's act of being. We must first grasp that a reality exists before we can know what it is. This is normal, for the intelligibility of reality is not ultimate. It remains wholly ordered to its act, its *esse*. We see how the famous distinction between *essence* and *esse* can only be understood at the metaphysical level in the light of this more radical division: being-in-act and being-in-potency.

The second mode of being-in-act is the good, which is realized fully at the level of the spirit, for a spiritual good is more perfect than all other goods (e.g., health, fame, wealth, etc.). The second mode of being-in-potency corresponds to this second mode of being-in-act: the affective power capable of loving the good, of undergoing its attraction, of letting itself be attracted by it. This second mode of being-in-potency is most perfectly realized at the level of the life of the spirit, the spiritual affective power (the will). This affective power is actuated in loving the good; it is actuated by it. In itself it is in 'expectation,' and it can only be understood in its essential order to a spiritual good which is its end.

In a particular individual (such-and-such a person) the will is clearly prior to the operation of love, yet the latter gives the former its true meaning. The power is made for love.

The third mode of being-in-act is that of truth. This mode, like the previous one, is realized at the level of the spirit, for truth is the end of the intellect; truth is the proper good of the intellect. The intellect most properly tends towards truth. The intellectual power capable of attaining to and living by truth corresponds to this third mode of act. The intellectual power is in itself completely ordered to truth which actuates it, perfects it, and allows it to be fully itself. Here also it is easy to understand that in every man, taken as an individual, the intellect, i.e., the capacity for reaching truth, and hence this power, is prior to truth. This power is only in act in perfect judgment.

The fourth mode of being-in-act is vital operation. This mode is only found in living beings. It is realized in them in different ways (think of the three degrees of life distinguished in man). The various vital powers of the different degrees of life correspond to this fourth mode of being-in-act. These vital powers are ordered to their operations which actuate them, complete them, and give them their full meaning. Here also the vital powers in man are prior to their operations.

Finally, the fifth mode of being-in-act is movement. This is the most imperfect mode, for movement is only the act of that-which-is-in-potency in so far as it is in potency. It is thus inseparable from the last mode of potency: mobile being. There is a reciprocal dependence between these two modes, a dependence that is in fact proper to physical being, which only exists in becoming. Consequently, the anteriority of a mobile being to its movement can be understood by the intellect, yet this mobile being cannot exist by itself and in itself – just as essence with respect to *esse* cannot, though in an entirely different fashion.

The distinction being-in-act, being-in-potency, therefore, takes up the major parts of philosophy (first philosophy, the philosophy of the spirit, the philosophy of the living being, and the philosophy of nature).

As soon as we grasp the anteriority of being-in-act to being-in-potency, we can conclude that everything in potency is ordered to and, in its being, depends upon being-in-act. This is the principle of final causality at the level of that-which-is considered from the viewpoint of being. At the level of being-in-act, this principle is grasped as the cause of causes. Consequently, a philosophy which has not attained being-in-act distinct from being-in-potency cannot attain the principle of final causality in its ultimate aspect.

Because there are five modes of being-in-act and being-in-potency, the principle of final causality in a metaphysical light can be expressed in five ways:

(1) Essence is ordered to and depends upon *esse*;
(2) Natural appetite is ordered to and depends upon a good;
(3) The power of intellectual knowledge is ordered to truth;
(4) All vital powers are ordered to vital operation;
(5) Mobile being is ordered to movement.

It can also be expressed in the following manner (in reverse order):

(1) That-which-is moved is moved by another;
(2) That-which-moves-itself moves itself by another;
(3) Judgment depends upon truth;
(4) Appetite is ordered to the good;
(5) All possible essence is ordered to *esse*.

ONE ('ONENESS')

After discovering the proper principle of that-which-is in the order of determination (substance) and its proper end (being-in-act), the philosopher must specify what 'one,' or 'oneness,' is and what 'many,' or 'multiple,' is, considered from the viewpoint of being. The question of one and many was of great importance throughout the whole of Greek philosophy. It continues to be a particularly important, complex problem, with different facets. In certain schools of philosophy the question is considered the central problem upon which all others depend. For Plato, as we have already said, beyond substance-being there is the Good-in-itself (*Bonum in sui*) and the One; similarly for Plotinus and Neoplatonism. It is the fundamental problem with Hegelian and neo-Hegelian philosophy. For Aristotle, on the other hand, the problem of one and many, while essential, is not primary. One is considered, as it were, the 'acolyte' of being, that which accompanies being and also manifests it. Many is the consequence of a particular mode of being: being-in-potency. These two totally different ways of seeing the relationship between one and being are very significant. If we identify being with the intelligibility of being, it is necessarily manifold, or many; and consequently, one must be prior to being, because many cannot be primary. Being is then relative to one. If, on the other hand, we recognize that the intelligibility of being is not being, then nothing prevents it from being prior to many and thus from being one; and nothing prevents one from being relative to being.

Let us reconsider the problem starting from experience and try to discern the connection between that-which-is and one, and that-which-is and many. It is true that we first experience many. The realities we see and feel are diverse and manifold. We ourselves are a complex reality, a 'cathedral of molecules' as the biologist would say. Our qualities and determinations are many; according to appearance, we are not a reality that is simple, indivisible, and one.

Nevertheless, we discover a certain deep oneness beyond manifold appearance. Is not every existent reality 'one' in its existence? Does it not have an originality which renders it irreducible to other realities? This is not something accidental: it is much deeper, it is what makes a reality such-and-such.

Thus, our experience of realities – in so far as it reaches sensible realities which are part of our universe – manifests above all the multiplicity of their determinations and their number. But our experience – in so far as it involves a judgment of existence, 'this is,' and attains to realities in their proper being – reveals to us the deeper unity, or oneness beyond their number and their complexity. We saw this with the induction of substance and act. It was unity in diversity which obliged us to go further to the discovery of a principle, an indivisible cause, source of the immanent unity in diversity. This indicates that the experience of many, of number, and even of the unity of realities, is never ultimate. When we reach the multiplicity of their determinations, their number, and also their existential and vital unity, we cannot stop. We must go further in order to discover what is beyond the existential and vital unity immanent to the diversity of determinations. In fact, the discovery of multiplicity does not come first (in the 'genetic' sense), for what we attain first is a particular form and quality. This is what first determines our knowledge. The affirmation of multiplicity and unity is secondary; it is doubtless very important, but it is neither primary nor ultimate. That-which-is can in fact exist in unity, individuality or, on the contrary, in multiplicity. There are simple realities and complex realities. These are two different ways of existing. Similarly there are lifestyles which tend towards simplicity and others which accept great complexity ... Language shows it clearly. We first of all assert 'this is,' and then 'this is one' or 'this is many.'

One and many thus appear as affecting existent reality, as manifesting its manner of being. They do not tell us what a reality is in itself, in its proper originality.

Let us further specify, by analyzing one and many in themselves, the relationship between one and many and that-which-is considered from the viewpoint of being. One is that which is not divided, and also that which is not divisible. We specify what one is by the negation of division: that which is 'beyond' division, which escapes division. Many is divisible, many is that which is divided. According to the genetic order, we grasp it before one, for it is closest to our conditioning, to our sensitive knowledge. It is involved in becoming. Becoming is in fact never simple; by nature it is manifold (the act of that-which-is-in-potency in so far as it is in potency). Yet according to the order of perfection, one is clearly before many, for the latter presupposes it, not the reverse. One directly affects being and accompanies it, manifesting its privilege of being undivided, not directly subject to division. Being, in itself, escapes division. So it is not surprising that, in order to grasp what one is, totally relative to being, we must consider it in connection with substance, principle and cause (in the order of the determinations) of that-which-is.

One manifests that substance is beyond the multiplicity of determinations and forms. One proclaims the independence, the 'autarky' of substance. Substance is undivided; it cannot be divided. Yet form is also undivided because it is (a) determination. What is the difference between the oneness of form and that of substance? It depends upon the form. It is easy to answer when it is the divisible form of quantity. Being divisible, quantity is not perfectly 'one'; it is only so in potency. Substance, however, is perfectly 'one.' It is 'one' in act. Quality is another question, because it is not a divisible form. It remains relative to substance. It is a 'disposition' of substance. Its oneness also remains relative to substance, whereas the oneness of substance is absolute. In order to understand the relative character of the oneness of form, we must understand that this oneness does not exclude multiplicity, while the oneness of substance does. Indeed, form-qualities are many, whereas substance is one, in the same existent reality. That is why oneness at the level of substance is not simply a formal oneness; it is a oneness of being. That of form, however, remains at the level of form; it is not at the level of being.

In connection with being-in-act, one manifests what is ultimate in being-in-act. As act, being-in-act is separated from that which is not being-in-act and is in itself undivided: it is one. Being-in-potency, on the other hand, is capable of being divided; it is the foundation of all multiplicity.

What is the difference between the oneness of substance and that of act? The former is fundamental; the latter is ultimate. The former is beyond all formal multiplicity; the latter is beyond all potentiality. It is by the negative aspect that we can express their distinction. We can also analogically affirm that, as substance is distinct from act, the oneness of substance is distinct from the oneness of act. One is the property of that-which-is considered as being, i.e., it is completely relative to it. At the same time, one manifests that-which-is. It leads us to the discovery of that-which-is, to the discovery of its proper principles. A property manifests the originality of a reality while being completely relative to it. As the 'acolyte' of being, one announces it and is relative to it.

Finally, let us point out that being-in-potency is the foundation of all multiplicity. Being-in-potency is capable of being divided, and so it is the source of all 'fractures,' all breaks at the level of being, life, and becoming.

THE HUMAN PERSON

These analyses of that-which-is considered from the viewpoint of being must help us grasp the 'how' of the most perfect being we experience – man – and so understand his manner of being, his person.

The human person is a complex individuated substance composed of a spiritual soul and an organic body. This helps us to understand his autonomy in the order of being and his individual oneness. The human person exists in himself and his great complexity is realized within deep unity. The human person also possesses numerous qualities which manifest his richness and perfection. We often judge the value of the human person by his qualities. By his qualities the human person shows his originality, his 'personality.' Every human person has a substantial autonomy, and each individual person also possesses various qualities and a special harmony between them. These qualities give him his own character and physiognomy – especially *habitus* progressively acquired in and through struggle.

The human person is likewise the seat of numerous relations, relations with the physical, vital and human world. Here too we often judge the value of the human person on the basis of his relations, and especially on his capacity for efficiency and irradiation – one might say, 'glory.' We are often tempted to look at a human person primarily in the light of his relations and his ability to communicate. This is of course the most conspicuous aspect, which manifests itself first. We like to define ourselves in terms of our friends, especially if they are illustrious and have great notoriety. But if we look more deeply, we understand that relations can only be specified by their foundation, and so by qualities and actions. Even more profoundly, we must arrive at substantial autonomy in the order of being.

This is the deep structure of the human person. It is an important aspect which allows us to grasp better what psychologists say about the human person, in particular about the three 'sentiments' of the ego or self: autonomy, self-esteem, and security. Autonomy of the self is based upon the radical autonomy of substance in the order of being. The sentiments of self-esteem and security are based upon natural and acquired qualities, and on relations.

Nevertheless, this aspect of a human person's structure is not enough to understand who or what the human person is; we must complete it with the metaphysics of act, for the human person is only perfectly himself when 'finalized,' that is, in communion with and brought to completion by his end. The human person is only finalized in loving another person, a human person chosen as a friend in reciprocal love. Spiritual love, however, requires knowing the friend. Spiritual love can only blossom when there is knowledge of the loved good. All accepted error diminishes love and fetters its development. The human person cannot be truly finalized without seeking truth and desiring truth; and this search for truth must constantly be renewed, for it is limitless. One can always go further.

This shows us how the human person cannot be enclosed within himself. A person implies welcoming another and giving to another. True communication happens through this reception and gift, and it requires an incessant search for truth.

Friendship assumes our vital operations, and involves progress, development, and becoming. Hence the human person implies growth. Although in his autonomy the human person implies an absolute, a determination, in his aspiration to love and seek truth, he also implies an *élan*, a limitless dynamism. This *élan* and dynamism occur in development, with its own rhythm of growth.

Hence we see what philosophy adds to inquiry into the human person, beyond what psychologists can say regarding him. In their analyses, psychologists show above all the 'genetic' development, or becoming of a person's behavior. They define neither his finality (end) nor his autonomy in the order of being. It is really with the discovery of end that we can explain the need for self-esteem and security. A 'finalized' spirit has self-esteem because it loves, and it acquires security when it attains truth. Truth liberates and brings deep security. Yet the philosopher knows that an end is not something acquired once for all. We strive for our end, we are attracted by it, and at each moment it unveils itself. It grasps us more and more profoundly. We struggle throughout our lives, and there can be setbacks. Not only does the human person remain vulnerable, but the more he develops, the more he becomes both stronger and vulnerable. He then understands better his possible 'brokenness,' those things that limit him in his appetite for the infinite.

9

THE SECOND STAGE OF FIRST PHILOSOPHY (WISDOM)[1]

The Discovery of the Existence of the First Being

The philosopher cannot stop at the discovery of the human person, wonderful as that may be. In order to be faithful to the search for truth and avoid any a priori (thus falling into intellectual laziness), he must pose a new question, the question to which all others lead: 'Is the human person the Supreme Reality? Is there another reality prior to the human person and to the universe?' The question is linked to the one that a philosopher must ask when confronted with ancient religious traditions and the affirmations of believers: 'Is there a reality that governs us and our universe? Is the God of religious traditions and believers a reality that the human intellect can discover? Or is he a myth to be denounced and, given that man cannot live at the level of myths, surpassed?'

We can see the importance of the question, for how it is answered deeply alters our outlook on the destiny of the human person. From a practical viewpoint, that of the orientation of our human life, it is paramount.

Nevertheless, we must recognize the difficulties encountered in trying to respond. We cannot have a direct human experience of the existence of a Supreme Reality, if it exists. Indeed, if it exists, it escapes us; it cannot belong to our universe.

However, can we say that we have an interior experience of it? If God exists, he is our Creator. He is, therefore, more present to us than we are to ourselves. . . .

Although we can have a certain interior experience of our soul – through our inmost vital operations (spiritual love, the will to love, the consciousness of our thoughts and reflections) – we cannot thereby discover the immediate presence of a Creator-God. Through the

1 See our study, *De l'être à Dieu. De la philosophie première à la sagesse* (Téqui, Paris 1977).

interior experience of our vital operations and reflection upon them, we discover something *lived*, something that remains in the immanence of our spiritual life. Can we, in and through this interior experience, go beyond the spiritual intentionality of these operations? Through the intentional form of these operations we do reach their spiritual existence, but we cannot claim, thereby, to discover the immediate presence of the Creator, for we remain in what is the fruit of our life at the level of the spirit.

Relying upon religious traditions, we can adore the Creator. We can then be conscious of this act of adoration and assert that it is intentionally addressed to a transcendent Reality in which we believe. It is belief in a Creator-God, however, that we acknowledge, not the intellectual discovery of his existence. An act of adoration presupposes the acknowledgement of a Creator-God, but does not reveal him.

Given the sharp criticism regarding the philosophical 'ways' (*via*) whereby the intellect seeks the existence of a First Being, and given the many atheistic ideologies that have developed over the past 150 years, we must be particularly attentive to this question.

Let us begin by specifying, from a critical viewpoint, that we cannot a priori refuse the possibility of the intellect discovering the existence of a First Being whom religious traditions call 'God.' We cannot a priori establish limits to philosophical inquiry. Indeed, if the intellect is truly ordered to that-which-is considered from the viewpoint of being, all that is can be either directly or indirectly reached by the intellect in its many and varied realizations. We may know nothing of the First Being, of what he most properly is, but we may perhaps be able to reach his being, his existence. If he whom religious traditions call Creator is the First Being, he is not totally indifferent to what we are, however transcendent he may be. He is the source of our being; so there must be a relation of dependence between us and him that we can perhaps grasp. To say a priori that our intellect is incapable of discovering the existence of this First Being is to limit beforehand the scope of inquiry of our intellect, to lock it into a particular category of being, a particular form of being. It is to cease looking at its fundamental relation to that-which-is as being. It is thus to refuse first philosophy.

Let us not forget that our intellect is actuated in knowing reality; it is not actuated by itself. By itself it is neither oriented nor determined; it is led by reality. Thus we cannot a priori establish a limit to its field of investigation; all we can say is that, at the present moment, our intellect has not yet discovered the existence of a transcendent Reality, the One whom religious traditions call God the Creator.

Secondly, major atheistic ideologies refuse the possibility that a First Being exists. Their pretext is the liberation of man. They consider God as man's rival, the antithesis of his liberty and the development of his life, creativity, and reason. These ideologies all have an idea of God which cannot correspond to the Creator-God, source of love, life, and being for man, as affirmed by the purest religious traditions. The refusal implied in this idea of God is perhaps only a nominal refusal of the true God who *is not* known. Or it may be a categorical refusal of all transcendent Reality; the rejection implied in these ideologies is then a real rejection of the true God, without any precise knowledge of him.

Lastly, if God exists, as the purest religious traditions say, he can only be Creator, First Being, Pure Act, the One who, from nothing, has communicated being to all that exists outside of himself. We can consider this as a philosophical hypothesis: Does this God really exist? Can I prove that he exists? Do the realities which I experience (myself included) correspond to this 'hypothesis'?

According to this hypothesis we can specify that the connection between Creator and creature can only be at the level of being, i.e., at the level of the act of being (*esse*), and not at the level of determinations, forms, qualities that we observe in ourselves, in other human persons, or in other living beings.

To this one could object that our intellect, our *cogito*, our freedom – all of which are spiritual qualities – allow us to be closer to God(-Spirit) than the mere grasp of the act of being common to all existent realities; and thus, through the spirit, we should be able to re-ascend to God most directly. Was this not Descartes' deep intuition, later taken up by Hegel? It is certainly very appealing; but is it possible? In reality we cannot directly grasp our spirit as spiritual substance; we can only grasp it through our spiritual operations of thought and will. The latter are reflectively grasped in their vital intentional mode, i.e., in their proper mode as creatures whereby they are completely different from God. God, the First Being in whom being and life are identical, is beyond this intentional mode. That is why we are obliged to recognize that only through the act of being, common to all that is, can we reach the First Being, the Creator – if he exists.

At the level of the act of being, however, there cannot be a reciprocal relation between Creator and creature. A creature receives everything from the Creator, who cannot be perfected by a creature. Consequently, we can only reach God using the principle of final causality.

It is thus only at the level of what is most proper to the act of being

— being-in-act reached by means of the judgment of existence and an induction beyond the judgment — that we can seek to attain to the First Being.

We cannot claim to discover the First Being immediately through the participated *esse* of a creature. The act of being, inasmuch as it is in a creature, is indeed what we call 'participated *esse*'; yet this act of being is not reached as 'participated *esse*.' We only reach participated *esse* in the light of the One who is '*Ipsum esse subsistens*,' just as we can only say that a reality is 'created' in the light of the Creator and the creative, or 'creating,' act. Claiming to discover the existence of the First Being through participated *esse* would be a *petitio principii*, i.e., 'begging the question.'

Similarly, we cannot discover the existence of the First Being, Creator through efficient causality, for in the realities that we experience we do not grasp their existence as an effect, but as a fact that imposes itself upon us. But we can pose the question, 'Whence does their act of being come?' According to our hypothesis we might answer, 'From the Creator, through the act of creation.' Yet we cannot grasp this act of creation starting from its proper effect (the act of being). As we have seen, that-which-is considered as being does not have a proper principle according to efficient cause. This is easily understood: that-which-is, in so far as it is, does not become, and thus, in so far as it is, it is beyond efficient causality. On the other hand the act of creation is God himself; there is no continuity between this act and its effect.

Thus the existence of the First Being can only be discovered through final causality at the level of being (this final causality implying efficient causality).

Furthermore, according to the admitted hypothesis, if God exists, our intellect cannot discover his existence through the mathematical sciences, the physical sciences, or the biological sciences. These sciences, remaining either in the realm of the possible or in search of relations of anteriority and posteriority, are not situated at the level of the act of being grasped in the judgment of existence. These sciences, therefore, can neither affirm that God exists nor say that he does not. They can merely indicate paths for research. They dispose and prepare; but they cannot lead us to discover the existence of the First Being. It is true that the more we see of the ordered complexity of the physical world, especially the world of living beings, the more we are led to affirm that it cannot have 'chance' as its source, and that there must exist some Organizing Thought. This, however, is not an argument, properly speaking. In and of themselves, the sciences do not call for or lead to it. They remain at the level of conditioning. Heidegger used to say they are at the level of *essent*, not of being. Let us say rather that they are at the level of conditioning and not of that-which-is.

We could make analogous remarks about all dialectical, phenomenological, or idealistic thinking which sets aside the judgment of existence. Such thinking remains at the level of ideas, the becoming of our intellectual life, what is lived (*vécu*) in our thought, and thus at the level of intentionality. Consequently, it cannot discover the existence of the First Being. Only realistic metaphysics which starts with the judgment of existence – 'this is' – and which discovers the priority of being-in-act to being-in-potency is capable of such inquiry. This is what can be said with the aforesaid hypothesis.

After these remarks from a critical viewpoint, let us see how we can answer the question: Does there exist a Reality beyond the human person? Let us see how the human intellect, from inquiry into that-which-is considered as being, is obliged to posit the existence of a First Being whom religious traditions and believers call 'God.'

This is a final effort of the intellect which questions existent reality and asks, based upon this reality, whether there exists someone who is the radical source and ultimate end of its being. Such an effort demands that we return to the various experiences of ourselves (the experiences that led to the development of the different parts of philosophy) and reconsider them from the viewpoint of the limit and actuality of their being. We do this in order to grasp the limits, the great metaphysical 'faults' or 'fractures,' of man's being, as well as his act of being. We understand thereby that man is not Being in the absolute sense. Instead, our metaphysical intellect must posit the existence of a Being, an ultimate Being, prior to man.

In order to go beyond man's being and discover the One who, beyond him, is the First Being, the intellect must be illumined by a grasp of being-in-act and its priority to being-in-potency. In this light the intellect penetrates our being and sees its limits at the level of being; it sees its potentiality. In the light of being-in-act we can discern the potentiality in our being and thus determine its limits.

I exist as I work, capable of transforming the physical world, transforming matter. In this transformation is shown my superiority over matter: I dominate it. Yet at the same time I depend upon it; it 'transcends' me, for it imposes itself upon me from without as a reality existing independently of me. I then see that I am not first in my being, because the being of the physical world is other and does not depend upon me. It imposes itself upon me. It is a given. Thanks to my capacity to have 'ideas,' to have 'forms' within me, I dominate the universe; I can transform it. Yet the universe is independent of me; it exists in itself. Thus there necessarily exists a Reality beyond my being and that of matter, for this duality requires a unity which transcends both me and the universe.

I exist as a friend, capable of loving a friend and of being loved by him. This reciprocal love, whose very reciprocity allows love to develop fully, manifests the natural love inscribed in my inmost being. There is a love that naturally 'carries' me towards the good, towards that which is capable of perfecting and fulfilling me. I thereby grasp the deep limit of my being, a being which does not have its proper end within itself, or possess its plenitude itself, but which needs to be ordered to another upon whom it depends and who is capable of attracting it. I also grasp what is most actual in me: the natural and ultimate love which unites me with my friend. It is evident, therefore, that I am not the First Being in my human person. The loved friend who attracts me is not the source of my being, for I, like him, am autonomous in my being. Consequently, there necessarily exists another Reality, beyond the human person, who is personal Goodness, a pure Spirit, in whom being and love are one.

I exist as capable of dying, of perishing, as having had a beginning in time. This indicates that my being is not pure act; it implies potency: it can or cannot be. Thus my being cannot be first. Yet because it *is* now in act, it depends upon another being who is Pure Act, for if he were not he would in turn depend upon another, and because we cannot go back *ad infinitum* in actual dependence in the order of being, this Other must necessarily be Pure Act, a Necessary Being beyond all potentiality.[2]

I exist as a living being, with vital autonomy, and an extremely complex organization that is nevertheless 'one.' I exist independently of other living beings and yet dependent upon the milieu in which I live. This indicates that there are limits in my living–being, yet also indicates that I live, that I am in act in my various vital operations. This act within me thus depends upon another Being in whom life and being are one.

Finally, I exist as part of the universe and as a moved being capable of transformation, of modification – for better or worse. Thus I am not

---

2 This impossibility of going back *ad infinitum* in actual dependence in the order of being cannot be proved; yet we can demonstrate that if rejected we meet with a contradiction, for if we claim to go back *ad infinitum* we must simultaneously affirm both the actual and possible character of this dependence.

first; I depend upon another who actuates me. I am a living being capable of moving myself, but in my deep, inmost being I am not the cause of my being, for in my becoming I am dependent upon the universe. Thus it is necessary to posit, beyond our universe and ourselves, another Being who is beyond movement.

In all five cases, it is always the same consideration: that which implies both act and potency in a being cannot be first in the order of being. It necessarily depends upon another who can only be a Being beyond all moved realities, beyond all potentiality. This Being is the One who attracts all the other realities which are moved and which are in potency, the One towards whom they tend.

THE MANNER OF BEING OF THE FIRST BEING

We can specify that this Act-Being who is Pure Act, Spirit, and Person, is none other than the Creator-God of religious traditions, because he is the One in whom there is no potentiality or dependence, and all that is not him is attracted to him.

To claim that the One whom we have reached in this manner cannot be God, the only Creator, that there is an abyss between the God of philosophers and the God of Christians, is to say that the human intellect cannot truly attain to the Absolute in the order of being, good, and life. As we have seen, we cannot claim this a priori. If, of course, the One whom we have discovered is 'infinite idea,' he cannot be God; for God is a spiritual reality, more real than all other realities. He is not an idea, the latter always being relative to what is before or after it and thus never first in the order of being.

The One who is discovered as Pure Act, Necessary Being, can only be a person, an absolutely simple spirit; this we can immediately affirm. In him there can be no potentiality (which matter, in itself, always implies). Thus he is separated and simple; in him there is no composition, for he is first. The appanage of the First is to be simple, without reference to another: he is himself.

This simplicity is in no way opposed to perfection or goodness, for it is the simplicity of the One who is the First Being and not an abstract, purely formal simplicity. It is the simplicity of an existent reality. It is the very simplicity of Being. Such simplicity is the very perfection of Being, for such a Being is not received into another. He is by himself and he possesses all the perfections of Being, Pure Act, and Spirit as well.

The First Being, Pure Act, has no limits. In his perfection and simplicity, he can only be infinite, in that his being, while completely determined (because Pure Act), is beyond every boundary. It is not opposed to anything; it is infinite in itself. It is an abyss of perfection and simplicity.

The First Being is beyond time; he is eternal. In him there is no becoming, no succession, for he is Pure Act. Everything in him is in a substantial moment, in the limpidity of the present with neither future nor past.

The First Being is alive, for to be alive is a perfection of being and not something secondary or accidental. Thus the First Being is necessarily a living being, or rather, he is Life, as he is Being. His life is that of a pure spirit, the simple life of spirit without composition, without bond to a body. It is the perfect life of the intellect and the will, contemplation and love.

This First Spirit, Pure Act, can have no object of contemplation other than himself — otherwise he would no longer be first. As the primacy of being requires simplicity, so the primacy of the spirit requires the direct contemplation of its own being, of its own goodness. The First Spirit thinks and contemplates himself. He loves himself, contemplating himself. Only in the First Being are love and contemplation substantially one. In his origin, his source, what he is, this spirit is light and love, indissolubly 'one.'

And it is in himself that he knows others and loves them. All is seen in the very limpidity of his contemplation, and all is loved in the depth of his substantial love.

THE CAUSALITY OF THE FIRST BEING

We must now specify the relationship between the physical universe — especially ourselves — and the First Being, Pure Act. It is a question that religious traditions and Judeo-Christian revelation have called 'creation': the creative act of God operating from nothing, *ex nihilo*.

If we compare the First Being with the existent realities we experience (including ourselves in so far as we exist), we can say that, with respect to the First Being, these realities can only be in a relation of total dependence in the whole of their being. Indeed, the First Being is absolutely simple in his being. He is pure Act, subsisting in his very act of being, absolutely autonomous in his own being. He is unique in the absoluteness of his act of being. Compared to him, all other beings are composite and, as they are not first, their act of being can only be participatory. The limits and complexity of our being were pointed out at the beginning of this inquiry. Compared with the First Being, we participate in the act of being. As the First Being is necessarily unique, all those who come after him are relative to him and participate in his being. Otherwise we would have to affirm that a being can limit itself in its being. A spiritual being can certainly limit himself in the development of his life: he can refuse to love; he can refuse to go beyond himself to meet one who is his good, his end, his fulfillment. This problem is proper to a spirit's freedom: he can withdraw and refuse to go further. Yet can we say that he is capable of limiting himself at the level of his substantial being? If this were so we would have to affirm that he gives himself his own substance, his own being, which he can increase or diminish as he wishes. Here again we find the question raised concerning the distinction between practical and theoretical knowledge. The question of freedom is not situated at the level of substance and being but at the level of human activities. For us, our being is a given which imposes itself; we have not given ourselves being. We are not the cause of ourselves – *causa sui* – at the level of substance and existence. If we do not admit this distinction we shall consider that, through freedom, we limit ourselves in our being. We shall consider freedom as *causa sui*, and opposed to dependence in the order of being. Is this not Sartre's problem? If our freedom is freedom of being, why are we still subject to death and suffering? If our freedom is freedom of being, then our neighbor, the other, enjoys the same freedom. But can there be two who have such freedom? Such freedom can accept no other freedom; another person hinders me from being the only one with such freedom. He must, then, be 'annihilated.'

If we acknowledge a limit to our being and that our being imposes itself upon us and does not come from us, we must then affirm that it comes from another, for being *per se* is primarily act; by itself it does not imply limit.

Yet we could claim that this limit is a trace of non-being in us and that such non-being is by itself a source of limit. Our being – which implies non-being – is thus limited and so the limit does not come from another ... It is true that our being fundamentally implies non-being, for it is limited; it is not pure being, pure act. But why does our being fundamentally imply this non-being? Because it is a limited being (all limit implies a negation).[3] However, the act of being fully determined by itself, does not imply non-being. Thus a limited being,

---

3 If we confuse limit and determination, we shall affirm that all determination involves a negation, is a negation and that, by this very fact, we are unable to distinguish between a created being and an uncreated being. Is this not the basic error of pantheism?

i.e., composed of being and non-being, depends upon another in its being. In a limited being, being is participatory. It depends upon a First Being who is Pure Act without non-being, without limit.

In a dialectical approach non-being is resorbed into being through becoming, in a completely immanent manner. In such a perspective, therefore, we need not say that the non-being present in being requires dependence upon another. But is it exact to say that non-being is resorbed into being through becoming? While becoming is genetically before being, being is before becoming in the order of perfection and end, and so becoming cannot explain the presence of non-being in being.

If all the realities we experience are limited, they participate in the First Being, and so receive their being from him. They are therefore radically caused by him, i.e., created. Participation in the order of being implies causality, for participation means 'receiving a share' in dependence upon another, partaking; when it is a matter of being, such dependence is what is proper to causality.

This first causality which comes from the First Being is obviously unique. It is completely different from all other causalities yet eminently contains them all, without having their limits; for this first causality is without limit. It cannot be limited. It can know no rivalry, for that which is other than the Creator comes from him and so proceeds from this causality and depends upon it, and consequently can neither oppose nor limit it. On the side of God, who is its source, this causality is infinite.

That is why we say that this causality occurs *ex nihilo*, i.e., unlike all other causalities which we experience, it does not cooperate with a pre-existent matter. Because it is first, nothing exists prior to it. Such a causality, as we have said, is not limited by a pre-existent matter. Thus it is not 'labor' but pure gift. It does not involve anything laborious, for nothing can resist it. It does not entail a struggle. It is a causality at the level of being and not at the level of form. It is a causality which is a pure gift of being, for all is given through this causality.

This causality is indeed absolutely free and gratuitous because it adds nothing to the Creator, to the First Being. The latter is infinitely perfect. He does not need to create to perfect or complete himself. Here again we catch a glimpse of the abyss separating this first causality from the causalities we experience, all of which perfect their agents or their causes because they actuate them and allow them to go beyond themselves. Even when we claim to love or work gratuitously, to do a completely gratuitous act, we only have the intention to do so. We do have the intention because we expect nothing from the one to whom we give or for whom we work; we do it as a pure gift, gratuitously. Yet, while this is true at the level of the motive of our activity, the activity itself perfects and fulfills us. It brings us something new which allows us to be more ourselves and, in this way, the activity — gratuitous as regards end — is not gratuitous as regards efficiency or exercise. Creative activity, on the other hand, is absolutely gratuitous, on the sides of both efficiency and end. The First Being does not create to perfect himself; he creates out of pure love, pure goodness. He loves Himself and, in loving himself, he wants to communicate freely what he possesses to others whom he creates, whom he 'places in being,' to whom he gives existence. His very activity as Creator modifies nothing in what he is; it actuates nothing in his proper being. It is an activity of superabundance, an activity that is pure gift.

Such an activity is, therefore, realized at the level of substantial goodness, a substantial love that can only communicate itself gratuitously; the created other only exists by means of such goodness and love from which he receives everything. Nevertheless, this other is loved for himself and only for himself, for he adds nothing to the perfection of his source.

Here we see the error of those who claim that the First Being creates out of necessity and that what he creates constitutes his completion. The first causality is then considered to be a necessary emanation, as though someone who is perfect is necessarily a source of communication: he necessarily engenders; it is his glory to engender and communicate. Is this not the perspective of the Stoics, of Plotinus and even that of Bergson? Such a perspective is understandable. However, is it not a projection upon the First Being of what we experience in our human life with procreation and art? In such a perspective, we do not see what is proper to the First Being, who, precisely because he is the First Being, is infinite and possesses in himself his proper perfection. To claim that the First Being creates out of necessity is to forget that being and spirit are one in him and that there can be no instinctive, biological necessity. If we speak of 'necessity' it can only be a necessity of superabundance proceeding from a supremely free act.

On the other hand, when we affirm that creative causality can in no way fulfill and perfect the First Being, that it is purely gratuitous, we must not, as a result, understand this causality to be that of a dilettante, of someone who simply plays, abandoning himself to chance. In considering creative causality in its absolutely free exercise, one might say that God, because he is God, creates in absolute freedom all that he wants, as he wants; he creates according to his 'fancy.' This is an incorrect conclusion. God creates all that he wills as he wills, according to his wisdom. Otherwise, it would no longer be a divine activity. Dilettantism and

fantasies are proper to man; they are proper to man tired of too wearisome
a duty, too severe a morality, and in need of some relaxation. They cannot
be proper to the First Being whose personal activity is to contemplate and
love himself, and who can only act in contemplating and loving himself.
A dilettante and fanciful God is no longer a Spirit-God. It is simply a
divinized imagination, a projection of our own imagination. While we
can say that God 'plays' when creating, such play is that of his wisdom, of
his wisdom's supreme liberty, but indeed *of his wisdom*.

The First Being, Pure Spirit, eternally contemplates and loves
himself, and it is in loving and contemplating that he decides to create.
This decision is the fruit of his light and his love; it is a luminous and
loving decision. It is made in total freedom, for it depends only upon
him. It has no other motive than his love, yet it is supremely wise, for it
is the fruit of his contemplation. It remains in the light of his
contemplation. Consequently, all that is willed and decided in this
creative act is eternal and is not in competition with the First Being,
Pure Spirit.

This decision is the first free act, fruit of the substantial love and the
substantial contemplation of God himself. This first free act is God
himself as Creator.

Furthermore, this free decision of God the Creator, fruit of his
contemplation – which in God is absolutely simple – is source of the
order of creation. While God is simple and unique, creation can only be
manifold; the reflection of the unity of the source can only be order,
harmony, marvelous rhythm.

The passage from One to many, from the unique and simple source to
its manifold and complex effects, was considered by Plotinus to be the
most difficult question for philosophy. One understands what he
means. Why did he who is One and absolutely simple, he-who-is,
decide to create, knowing full well that One would thereby have to
accept multiplicity, that One would no longer be alone, that *many*
would appear? By his creative act was he not going to destroy unity and
perfection? Was he not necessarily accepting many, that which is
imperfect and thus, in the final analysis, evil? Does this creative act,
which brings about the transition from One to many, from light to the
opaqueness of matter, not imply a certain complicity with evil? Can
such an act really be the fruit of free love and thus good? Is it not rather
a necessity which imposes itself: God cannot remain alone, and, as he
cannot create other gods, he necessarily creates limited spirits capable
of rebelling, capable of refusing love? Does he not necessarily create
matter, source of all opaqueness and of all limits?

We cannot avoid addressing this problem, which remains a mystery for the philosopher. Evil seems to overcome good in creatures. Spiritual creatures seem to ignore their creative source, even to rebel against it. They become tyrannical towards their fellow creatures ... and God keeps silent before these injustices! If he is a God of love who has created everything out of love, how can he tolerate what we ourselves find intolerable? Thus the question of evil is posed. Was God not an accomplice of evil in creating? He knew, when creating spirits, that these spirits were both too great and too small – infinite as spirits and limited as creatures – and that they would rebel against Love, against their Creator, and would become tyrants with an evil conscience.

In order to respond, we would have to penetrate the secrets of God. The philosopher cannot. He can only ascertain what exists and what he experiences. Through what he experiences he can recognize the necessity of positing a First Being, Pure Spirit, and recognize that this First Being is indeed the Creator. He can also recognize, as we have seen, that the Creator's creative act is absolutely free and can only be decided out of love and in love, luminous love. The philosopher can thereby try to remove the scandal and respond to Plotinus. The primary intention of the One who creates out of love and in the light of his contemplation is not to destroy unity; it is not to look at multiplicity. His primary intention is to communicate his love and his goodness by gratuitously communicating being. To create is to communicate being. Creation is the gift of being which, as the Neoplatonists said, has different degrees of perfection: *esse, vivere, intelligere.*[4] What is important to underscore is this primary intention: love. A creature is indeed limited in its participatory being and thus, by this very fact, complexity and multiplicity appear. Complexity and multiplicity are, as it were, a *sine qua non* condition for participatory, communicated being, though not willed for themselves. If we consider them first, we are trapped in a dialectical opposition; but this is not so if we situate them as a necessary condition for a creature. Thus evil is not directly willed, but it can occur. God creates spirits in his love and he creates them free; hence they can rebel and refuse love. This is not directly willed by the Creator, however. He only wants to communicate love.

One might object that God knows the fragility of his spiritual creatures. He knows that they will lack the love necessary not to rebel, and thus he should not have created them. Is it not a lack of prudence to create masterpieces who end by destroying themselves?

God does not create spiritual creatures so that they might destroy

4 Being, living, thinking.

themselves. He creates them so that in loving and being faithful they might be perfectly themselves and glorify their Creator. Nevertheless, he leaves them free, and allows them to go astray. Is this not incredible magnanimity rather than a lack of prudence? The question is whether or not love is what is most precious. We then understand the incredible risk of love which calls for love. This love, being lucid, knows the risk of a break. The risk is entirely assumed into and by love. In the end, it is only this love which enables us to go beyond the scandal we feel when we have the impression that evil predominates in spiritual creatures and defeats the good. Quantitatively, as regards what we can measure, this is true, but qualitatively it is not, for the Creator permits evil so that freedom can be safeguarded and an act of love occur. This clearly shows the inestimable value of love in the eyes of God's wisdom. Yet we have difficulty in conforming ourselves with this judgment, for we judge from outside and primarily see the consequences of human activities. Unlike God, we do not see from inside.

The creative causality is indeed the fruit of contemplation and love, and it gratuitously and directly reaches the being of all that is, fulfilling an order of wisdom in all that it does.

This causality is exercised with no becoming and no intermediary. It is immediate. That is why all that is other than the Creator depends entirely upon him in its very being. This is what is meant when it is called a 'creature.' While that-which-is exists, while it possesses a certain autonomy in its substantial being – it is a particular reality with a particular determination, with its own particular intelligibility – it nevertheless remains totally dependent in its act of being, its existence, upon God's creative act. It is certainly not defined by this act, but a creature is entirely dependent upon God's creative act in its existence. Here we must avoid two extreme positions:

1. The first consists in saying that a creature's being can only be understood relative to that of the Creator (the ontological position of Malebranche). This position is untenable and contrary to experience. It is not by starting from God, whom I do not experience, that I grasp and know both physical reality and myself. In this perspective a creature has neither its own intelligibility nor any autonomy. The only autonomous being is the Divine Being. Being is then immediately divided into finite and infinite being, where finite being is completely relative to infinite being and only intelligible through it. In this case, metaphysics is absorbed by theology.

2. The second consists in saying that a creature's participatory *esse* is

accidental; it is adventitious to its essence, its being, which can be perfectly conceived without its *esse*. We must therefore first conceive the essence of realities and have some idea of them, before asking whether or not they exist. The essence of created realities is separated from their participated *esse*, which becomes for them a type of exterior covering (the perspective of Avicenna, Ockham, Descartes, and Kant). Metaphysics becomes the metaphysics of essences, of the possible and no longer of that-which-is.

In the first of these perspectives, the judgment of wisdom, the ultimate judgment of metaphysics (a judgment in the light of the creative act), is identified with the judgment of existence which is at the starting point of metaphysical inquiry. In the second, our intellect remains as if enclosed within its own conditioning — the abstraction of essences — and that-which-is is grasped from it.

Here we see the difficulty in specifying the exact relationship between our intellectual knowledge, which primarily attains to that-which-is in its act of being, and the intellectual knowledge which ultimately reaches the existence of First Being, Creator of this same reality. The same existent reality must be considered under two different aspects: in itself — as reached by our intellect — and in its dependence upon the creative act, upon the Creator, in so far as it possesses participatory *esse*.

The creative act, source of participated *esse*, immediately reaches all that is, outside of First Being, in its inmost, deepest being. Thus we must distinguish the question of creation from that of biological evolution. Without passing judgment on the proper character of biological evolution, or on the way in which it must be conceived, note that to claim that evolution is opposed to creation is to confuse what is most proper to being and the way in which biological life develops. We must understand that the creative act directly concerns participatory *esse* and not life, *a fortiori* life as the biologist considers it, i.e., in its conditioning. Precisely speaking, God's creative act concerns participatory *esse* in all created realities. Among these there are those who are more perfect than others, to which the Creator has communicated life in its various forms.[5] The Neoplatonists had already distinguished between God the Creator who gives *esse* and God the Father who

5 In speaking here of God's creative act which concerns *esse*, we are taking the creative act in its proper sense, which is to produce *ex nihilo* and thus without use of any instruments. When we speak philosophically of Father-God who communicates life, we are speaking of an act of God that can make use of instruments because life is not first; it always presupposes the creation of *esse*.

communicates life. Although to live is to be for a living being, at the philosophical level our intellect distinguishes between the *esse* and the *vivere* of a living being. Moreover, evolution is at the level of the *conditioning* of biological life. This evolution is not adequate to life considered as life. Life itself cannot be reduced to *esse*. Thus there can be both biological evolution and creation; there is no contradiction.

PROVIDENCE AND DIVINE GOVERNMENT

Associated with the question of creation is the question of Providence and the government of the First Being. This question, first considered by the Stoics and Neoplatonists, took on major importance with the Fathers of the Church and later theologians. It is encountered again in Leibniz; and Hegel's philosophy of history is, ultimately, a sort of secularization of this theological question.

This question can be developed in philosophy at two different levels: the physical universe considered in its totality, and man, a spiritual creature endowed with freedom. God thought the universe as he created it. He thought it in his wisdom as he ordered it, realizing in it an order of reciprocal causalities, a hierarchical order of perfection in the various physical creatures, animate or inanimate. The order which the physical and biological sciences seek in physical and biological realities is, as it were, an echo, a reflection of the profound order of divine wisdom. The order which the philosopher also seeks in his consideration of the universe and the living being is the proper effect of divine wisdom. It is precisely because the universe was created by and in God's wisdom that it possesses such profound and harmonious intelligibility.

Having created the universe in his wisdom, God preserves and governs it. In his vision everything in the universe is intelligible. He creates and preserves it. Matter itself has no opaqueness for God because it is the fruit of his thought. Nevertheless, the fact that our universe is thought by God does not mean that it is perfectly determined and that in it there cannot exist any deformity, accident, or brokenness. God willed to create it with its matter, and the latter is the source of indetermination, of potentiality. God willed it so. While chance does not exist for God (he knows matter's 'failures' or 'abnormalities'), for us something will always escape our most advanced scientific and technical knowledge, because we shall never be able to eliminate matter, that radical element of indetermination willed and created with our universe by God.

Affirming that God foresees everything in our universe and governs it does not mean that it must be perfectly and completely determined, with no deformity, no fracture. What we must understand is that the deformities and fractures are known and permitted for the sake of a superior equilibrium, a more elevated order of the universe as a whole and, in the end, for the sake of man.[6] Thus, in the perspective of God's wisdom, what we call physical evil, physical disorder, privation of order, of a particular form is directed to a higher order which escapes us, for we can never grasp the order of the universe in its totality.

Could God have created a more perfect universe? A negative answer cannot be given, for God created it freely and according to his wisdom. We can say, however, that he governs it with unique intelligence. We cannot assert that God could govern the universe with greater wisdom.

In the case of man, who is a spiritual creature, we can say that God in his wisdom does not regard and govern him primarily as a part of the universe — as he does its material parts — but for man himself (God looks at man for himself). Man has a personal end willed by God. Man possesses a spirit, and by this spirit he is no longer part of a whole, but is in himself a 'whole.' It can also be said that God created and governs the physical universe for the sake of man. The physical universe has no other end than its most eminent part: man who possesses a spirit. According to God's wisdom, matter can only be for the spirit, as becoming is for being. To consider man as only a moment in the evolution of our universe — and hence a moment which must disappear — is to forget that matter is a proper principle not of being but of becoming, and that the spirit is essentially defined as relative to being and not becoming.

If the entire physical universe is ordered to man, then man is the masterpiece of the Creator and, in a unique way, he is the object of his providence and government. Indeed, having a spiritual soul, a spirit, man receives from God the ability to think, to love, to organize and direct himself. God is Father in the strongest sense because he communicates to man a spiritual life, a life of light and love. As this communication takes place in love, God infinitely respects the spiritual soul, the spirit he created. He loves it as he loves himself. He directs, attracts, inspires, and enlightens it, respecting it in its own exercise of its biological laws and spiritual conditioning. And God leaves man free to choose. He therefore accepts that man may freely turn away from him and forget him in order to look only at that which is immediate,

6 Christian theology would say: for the sake of man's salvation.

sensible, closer to his conditioning. The providence and government of the Creator do not tyrannically impose themselves upon man with pressing necessity. The Creator governs man as one governs with love an intelligent being capable of orienting itself. God, therefore, allows this being to turn in on itself with pride. He permits faults. Yet one might ask whether this is really a good way of loving. Is it not in reality a poor way, a weakness? Through his fault man destroys himself and turns away from his true happiness. God who loves him should not allow this! Is there not a certain tacit complicity of God in this permission, and thus a lack of love?

To say this, however, is to forget that, having willed to create a spirit capable of thinking and loving, God cannot force him to love. To allow fault in a spirit is not weakness but rather fundamental respect – the exigency of the love that created the spirit. Forcing a spirit to love is to destroy him as spirit; it is to do him violence. When God creates a spirit, he respects the spirit's nature. He governs him as a spirit, and thus commits himself to him and leaves him the possibility of turning away. To do otherwise, God would betray his own work.

To claim that to allow preventable evil is to be an accomplice to such evil and, consequently, that if God allows fault he could prevent he is an accomplice to fault, is to fail to understand that the situation of the Creator with respect to a created spirit is entirely different from that of our will before the evil we encounter. We always act from without. God acts directly and intimately upon all created spirits from within. Thus, if we can stop evil we must make every effort to do so, knowing that we shall be responsible for it if, able to stop it, we let it happen out of negligence or a false conception of freedom. But God cannot prevent fault without destroying man's freedom. It is astonishing to realize that the One who acts in love in such an intimate way is, by that very fact, the One who most respects the other and, out of love for him, cannot prevent him from doing evil. We have some sense of God's situation when we are closely bound in love to a friend and this friend begins to do 'stupid things' . . . Someone less bound in love might admonish him more easily. If we sense that we must remain silent, it is not out of weakness but rather to safeguard a higher good. This, of course, is only a distant likeness. With God the Creator the situation is infinitely more profound, for his love is first, substantial and unique. Consequently, God is, as it were, 'bound' to his spiritual creature and cannot prevent him from doing evil, for he loves him and infinitely respects his freedom. God can warn the spiritual creature. He can educate him. God, however, cannot take away the freedom his spiritual creature has to act against and disobey him, to exalt himself falsely in pride.

When a philosopher considers God's creative act, the gaze of God-Providence and the attentiveness of his government over man, his masterpiece, he understands that the only true response of a spiritual creature is to acknowledge his dependence freely and lovingly and adore his God and Father. Indeed, if the creative act reaches us deeply in all that we are, if our entire being is the effect of the Creator-God, if our spiritual soul is immediately created by him, God is intimately present to what we are. There is no distance between him and us; there is a unique, substantial, intimate contact. The Creator-God, the immediate source of my entire being and my spiritual life of light and love, is more present to me than I am to myself. Let us be precise: I am only conscious of being present to myself by reflecting upon my activities of thought and love; that is why I am present to myself in a consciousness that can only be intentional, although this presence is certainly rooted in a substantial interiority beyond all intentionality. Hence I seek to go beyond the intentional mode in order to grasp the deeper aspect of my spirit. In silent reflection, I can – beyond all acts of thought and love – try to grasp the intimate and hidden source of my activities, although I can never perfectly and directly grasp it in its being, its substantial being, beyond all its effects. I can certainly wish to go beyond these effects in reflection, but they always remain present. It is indeed by going beyond them – and so still being in them – that I reach a deep interior silence which places me in the presence of what I am as spirit. God the Creator, on the other hand, is present as the primary, substantial source, as the loving source that never ceases to give itself and carry everything that comes from it. Nothing is outside of God; nothing is considered by him in an exterior fashion. Everything is grasped in and through him, in his light and love. Yet I do not experience this presence; I affirm it in a judgment of wisdom. And normally I seek to be as attentive to it as possible. It is through an act of adoration, a voluntary act of love, that I dispose myself to being as attentive as possible to this presence and that I bring about silence within myself. It is a completely different silence from that which makes me attentive to myself, for the latter occurs in reflection which takes me beyond my acts to be attentive to their immanent source. The silence of adoration, however, is an act of love, an act of gratitude with respect to the One who gives me everything and who keeps me. This voluntary act of love lays hold of me in all that I am, so that I offer myself to the source of my being, my life, my light, and my love. Hence we discover a new dimension in man's being, that of the religious man who acknowledges himself as loved with unique, eternal love, and who responds to this love in an offering of self. The religious man acknowledges God the Creator as first, and sees himself as receiving everything from him.

Contrary to what some have said, this religious dimension does not alienate man, nor does it diminish him and place him in a state of inferiority, dependence, or slavery. The acknowledgement of dependence is not necessarily or inevitably an alienation. While dependence upon an inferior reality is indeed true alienation, true enslavement, the acknowledgement of our dependence upon the source of our being, life, and spirit is, on the contrary, true liberation, for it is to return to the source. Now such a return is always salutary, especially when this source is the source of light and love. If God were our rival, it is clear that to adore him and place ourselves in dependence upon him would lead to our destruction. But the true God cannot be a rival; he is the unique source of our entire being. Thus, this radical return to God in love and freedom through adoration places us in the most fundamental practical truth: we have received everything from him and we radically depend upon him alone.

Our response to the creative act of God must not only be one of adoration, but as far as possible, one of contemplation as well. We do not, of course, see our Creator; nevertheless, he is present to us, giving himself to us. Through his proper effects we can seek to deepen our knowledge of his goodness and love, and to elevate ourselves to him. This contemplation is always mediated by the realities we know and can look at as actual 'reflections' of his power, wisdom, and goodness. These realities – his creatures – veil him from our eyes yet render him present. They manifest him. We must, therefore, choose from among these creatures those which manifest him best. First among these is the order found in the universe, whether it be the infinitely vast order of stars and galaxies, or the living beings around us, part of our terrestrial universe. Also, among such creatures, there is the order of the life of our spirit, our intellect and loving will, what we discover in our search for truth. Our intellect in its most profound aspect is entirely ordered to its source. Without knowing its name it cries out to it and is wholly attentive to it. In our intellect is a natural appetite for being, and thus for the hidden source of all that is. Our will seeks to love. When it loves a friend, the love which is bound to that of the friend helps us grasp the presence of the One who has created us in love and who gives us the capacity to love. The grandeur of the human person discovered in love better reflects God the Creator than all that can be discovered in the order of the universe. We might call it a living image of God the Creator, for through this loving presence we are close to the One who is primarily the Person-Friend. So radical is love for God (it is primary) that every other love is enveloped by it, and while it cannot be reciprocal – there cannot be a natural friendship between man and his Creator – it nevertheless awaits our response. The silent presence of God the Creator is so active and so 'present'[7] that it makes use of all that comes from him to remind us silently that he is there. Nevertheless, this presence is diametrically opposed to an encroaching, stifling presence, for, as the radical basis of our autonomy and our liberty, it remains veiled.

Thus man cannot be content to 'think Being' and passively wait for God (if he exists) to come and meet him. He must, having discovered that he exists, adore him and seek to be as close to him as possible by contemplating him through his effects and images.

THE JUDGMENT OF WISDOM

Thanks to this contemplation, a philosopher can have a new perspective on himself and all that he seeks to know. This perspective is really a gaze, a vision 'of wisdom,' for it occurs in the very light of God the Creator. The philosopher can thereby encounter what is correct in both the ontologist and existentialist perspectives. For this new vision considers man in the light of the love the Creator has for him. It also considers man as a creature, in his existence as creature. A contemplative person can grasp in himself the following truths:

1. There exists in his very being a profound and radical 'fracture,' for his act of being is received and distinct from what he is in his essence. Thus, in man, there is a radical potentiality with respect to his act of being which means that he could *not* be. In a certain sense non-being precedes his act of being. If man did not consider God's creative act he would fall into anxiety, because in man there is the possibility of not being. If he did not see himself as dependent upon the creative act, the possibility for non-being would be a source of

7 If we are attentive to the expression from contemporary philosophy, 'Nothingness annihilates,' which expresses a type of active hold of Nothingness upon our being (in other words, in a vision of wisdom: upon limited, created being), we discover here the dialectical antithesis of God's creative presence. The creative presence of God 'presents' itself, realizes itself as a presence, i.e., it is one with God's creative action upon which it is based, unlike all other presences, for which action is only the basis of presence and from which, consequently, the former is always really and formally distinct.

vertigo, the vertigo of nothingness. If we forget a contemplative
vision we can end in anguish from nothingness, an anguish which
seizes us in all that we are.

2. There is a previously unfathomed depth to his created spirit which a
   contemplative philosopher can grasp in the light of the creative act,
   a spirit capable of re-ascending to its Creator by means of his
   intellect, a spirit capable of loving, adoring, and contemplating his
   Creator. There is an infinite appetite in a created spirit for knowing
   truth and for loving, an appetite which nothing outside of God can
   satisfy. The human intellect has an infinite capacity ordered to the
   First Being, God, and the will has a spiritual appetite ordered to the
   ultimate Good, God. This explains the freedom so deeply inscribed
   in our inmost will. Yet it is not this freedom which places our will
   closest to God; it is our spiritual appetite for loving. The freedom
   inscribed in our will, while it can be at the service of a spiritual love
   for God, can also set itself in opposition, in an attitude of refusal.
   We are capable of exalting ourselves in our capacity to think, in our
   radical autonomy, and withdrawing and turning away from God. In
   our spirit there will always exist a capacity for refusal, a capacity to
   make an absolute of the negation of love, thereby exalting ourselves.

3. We can also grasp in the light of the creative act that our spiritual
   soul cannot disappear after death; it has something immortal. This
   can be understood from the fact that our intellect is capable of
   adoring God the Creator and contemplating him. There is an
   essential 'order' in our spirit as regards God and, consequently, our
   spiritual soul can exist beyond our corporeal conditioning. The soul
   is, indeed, the form of the body, but it possesses in itself a depth of
   being which enables it to emerge beyond the organic body. Our soul
   is not only the form of our body. It possesses a natural, fundamental
   'order' towards an ultimate spiritual end: God. This order is not
   only an intentional order at the level of vital operations, but a
   substantial order. This enables us to assert that our soul, because it
   is spiritual, cannot disappear with death. What will be its manner of
   being and living after death? The philosopher cannot say, but he can
   assert that the human soul, in its proper substance, does not
   disappear after death; it is immortal.
      If the soul is immortal, it is necessarily created directly by God. It
   is created by God to inform a body which was biologically
   conceived. To be precise: if the soul is immortal, it necessarily

depends upon God's creative act even though God does not take the initiative. God responds to the initiative of the parents; he cooperates with a man and a woman in the work of procreation. At the level of philosophical reflection we cannot state the precise moment at which man's soul is created by God to inform the body biologically conceived and developing in the maternal womb; it is probably at conception. But we can affirm that as soon as there is conception at the biological level, the creative Wisdom of God is engaged to create – at a time that God decides – a spiritual soul to inform and assume a new living being, allowing it gradually to become a human person. That is why a human being is present from the moment of conception; he is biologically present with his 'program.' He is present with his spiritual soul either in act or in real 'expectation,' according to the proper intention of divine wisdom.

4. In the light of the creative act we can better grasp how work – noble as it may be – cannot be man's end, for we see that man's ultimate end is God. Moreover, work is not cooperation with the creative act in the precise sense, although it does bring to completion the work of the Creator. By his intellect, man has the capacity to dominate the physical universe and transform it. How far will man be able to go in this transformation? He can modify the 'figure' of this world, the 'face' of this world, and modify its forms; but he cannot attain to that profound being which only the creative act of God reaches. Man always works upon pre-existent matter, transforming it from without; however, he cannot suppress it. Here we must be attentive to the different meanings of the word 'matter' in philosophy and science. We are speaking of matter in the philosophical sense and not in the scientific sense. What is certain is that man, a spiritual and religious creature, can glorify his Creator through his artistic activity; he then places his artistic work at the service of his religious activity. This is how liturgical art is born.

5. In the light of the creative act we can understand better that friendship is not the ultimate end of human activity but an intermediate end. Man must develop in himself a religious dimension that gives new intensity to his ethical activity and opens a new field for it. The religious activity of adoration – whose fruit in our will is the virtue of religion – is a fundamental activity that irradiates or influences all our other human activities, even friendship. Indeed, a friend is no longer only respected for himself,

because he is loved, but because he is loved by God with a personal love and respected by God in a unique way. The virtue of temperance can experience new demands, even to the extent of consecration of one's entire self to God (the spirit of virginity) in order to be more free for contemplation. The virtue of fortitude can also experience a new intensity, even to the extent of the offering of our life in order to be faithful in our adoration of the one true God; the fortitude of a martyr is rooted in the virtue of religion. The virtue of justice, deepened by the sense of our dependence upon God, develops to the point where we efface ourselves in humility before others who possess qualities that we do not. It also develops in reparation for the injustice committed against God by our faults of pride. The virtue of penance can only be born under the influence of the virtue of religion. Prudence finds itself relativized by the demands proper to adoration and contemplative wisdom.

Thus the harmony of human life is transformed by adoration and contemplation. We discover a new dimension of anthropology, that of the religious man who acknowledges his dependence as creature upon his Creator. Such anthropology considers the religious man: a man who adores, a contemplative man, a man capable of going beyond himself and offering his life to glorify his Creator and bear witness to the Creator's unique love. This new depth in man's heart – his religious and contemplative capacity, his capacity to love his Creator in adoration and contemplation – is a response to God's first and gratuitous love, a response in which man acknowledges a fundamental covenant with the Creator.

6. We can also relativize man's political dimension, while maintaining its nobility. We can better understand the danger of the primacy of politics, the absolute primacy of community over person. The primary covenant is indeed that of man with his Creator, followed by that of man with man in friendship. In order to discover these two covenants and live them, man must accept his human condition, which implies a becoming and a communal life in which he can be educated and develop his human qualities. Man must therefore acknowledge the demands of the family, those of the various communities of life, and, lastly, those of the political community. In the light of these considerations he acknowledges that he must go beyond the common good of the family and the political community in these two ways: adoration – and all religious activity *per se* – and friendship. The familial and political communities must respect both the religious and the personal demands of

man. It is not up to them to regulate these demands, nor to order
them, for these demands surpass the familial and political communities; these communities must acknowledge and respect them.

The development of religious activity – adoration and contemplation – gives a more acute sense of the human person and his radical
autonomy. In and through his spiritual soul, man depends upon his
Creator alone and can be personally bound to him. This opposes all
political socialization. There can be no formally religious politics.
The family, however, is directly transformed by the religious
covenant between man and God, for the question of procreation is
not considered in the same way when the spiritual soul is understood to be created directly by God. This primary covenant between
man and God gives the family a more fundamental autonomy.

7. Finally, in the light of the creative act, we can consider the entire
    physical universe as created by God and, therefore, as possessing a
    unity willed by his wisdom. Was this universe, which is radically
    dependent upon God, created from all eternity or in time? The
    philosopher cannot say. He can only advance a suggestion, saying
    that it seems more fitting for the universe to have been created in
    time, given that it seems to possess its own specific rhythm ... but
    he cannot affirm this absolutely as a metaphysical truth or a truth
    arising from a judgment of wisdom.

    Faced with the question of the eternal First Being, we can better
    grasp the meaning of time, the reflection of eternity in our physical
    universe. The Platonic and Neoplatonic vision of time as the 'image
    of eternity' must be kept in a vision of wisdom. The same applies to
    physical movement, the act of that-which-is-in-potency in so far as
    it is in potency. Is not movement a sort of vestige in the physical
    world of the rest and silence of divine contemplation?

    In the light of the creative act of the First Being, there is an
    ultimate judgment upon the meaning of matter. If God willed to
    create a physical world, is it not so as to communicate more love? If
    the creative act were only an act of light and intellect, God would
    have only created pure spirits; but because this act is above all a
    gratuitous act of love, we can understand how pure potentiality
    (matter) allows love to manifest its gratuitousness. Is matter not, as
    it were, a great symbol of the poverty of a creature who is pure
    receptivity in the presence of its Creator and Father? What is
    greatest in a creature is, indeed, its radical, substantial potentiality,
    its capacity for waiting (it is wholly 'expectation' with respect to its
    Creator), for peaceful waiting, because it is in the Father's hands.

Matter, in its most radical aspect, is the foundation of all expectation, all desire, all hope, and these perhaps best characterize a
creature as such (whereas fidelity characterizes a created spirit).

8. God alone is the hidden source of life, whose greatness we also
   grasp, and this explains why life in the physical universe arises in
   such a hidden and veiled way, imperceptible to our eyes and to
   scientific investigation. The origin of life always remains hidden
   from human eyes. As though to show us the infinite tenderness of
   his love, God communicates such a great gift without show,
   without tension. It is a hidden communication, veiled by matter,
   yet occurring by means of the material world which preserves it and
   allows it to develop in so extraordinary a fashion. It is not being that
   is veiled, but life. Life is veiled by matter which is not (in itself) life.
   The latter can only be unveiled in and through the spirit in which it
   becomes conscious. By means of his spirit, man is the guardian of
   life; he is the 'shepherd of life.' Life – communicated at its origin in
   such a hidden way – develops magnificently up to the creation of the
   spiritual soul. The spiritual soul is also hidden at its origin, yet it is
   capable of proclaiming the grandeur of life. Life can be manifested
   with the spirit; it can be unveiled with splendor.
   Yet is not the living being necessarily, of itself, the source of life?
   A living being endowed with biological life involves an alliance
   between life and matter. The latter allows created life to be fruitful,
   and this fruitfulness allows God, the Father of life, to be still more
   hidden, for a living being then appears as the proper source of life. A
   living being is the proper source of life in its fruitfulness, but not its
   primary and ultimate source. For this reason the philosophy of the
   living being cannot enable us to discover the existence of God
   directly. A living being hides the existence of its primary source.
   Once again we discover how matter allows greater communication
   of love, for it allows love to communicate itself as the source of life
   and fruitfulness. The discovery of this fruitfulness, while it does not
   allow us to discover the existence of its primary source, places us in a
   state of admiration and expectancy; for chance cannot be source of
   fruitfulness, only love can be that. This fruitfulness, while veiling,
   reveals the primary love of the Creator. It gives his presence without
   manifesting or saying what he is. Indeed, the fruitfulness of life is
   beyond words, beyond *logos*, for it is an untamed, gushing source.

While God is the primary, hidden source of life, he is also the Master
of death, at least as regards man's death, for to man he has entrusted the

terrible power of killing. Man can tyrannize living beings which are inferior and subject to him (animals and plants), and he can destroy them. This power cannot legitimately be extended to his fellow man, however, except in the case of lawful defense. For each man has the same dignity, and each living soul, having been created directly by God, is in the hands of God. Thus human life must be respected, for it belongs not to man but to God, God alone. With inferior living beings, however, life is transmitted by secondary causes without the special intervention of God the Creator. God wanted these 'relays,' so that man should be left with the power to intervene and modify their rhythm.

It is understandable that man should feel a sort of sacred trembling before the power to destroy the life of inferiors, and be horrified at destroying that which is smaller than himself. This sentiment, although noble, lacks realism; for if God has given this power, it is so that man can understand better that only life bound to spirit is sacred, that only man's life is sacred. But this power must not blind man to the point that he thinks the progress of science and technology give him a right to decide the extent of his power over the life and death of his fellow man – as if he himself were the master of his life and death, and that of his fellow man. When he believes himself to be judge and master he usurps the place of the Creator. He can do so unconsciously – not having discovered the existence of the First Being, the Creator – but this does not make it any less a gesture of great insolence, for man must at least respect what is beyond him, what he does not know. If he is honest with himself, he must discern what is hypothetical in his research and what is discovered scientifically or philosophically. The origin of life, the origin of man, remains a hypothesis. Man has no right to evade the problem; he must face it, understanding that life in its depths escapes him, that the spirit escapes him. Consequently, he must suspend judgment and wait. What is most fundamental in man remains unknown to him: his own origin, the first moment of his life, his extreme weakness at the moment of conception. He must, therefore, respect this state in his fellow human beings lest he destroy himself; for he is incapable of fully assuming himself.

What is true of the first hidden moment of life, the first embryonic moment, is true of the final and ultimate moment, that of death. It too remains hidden (we speak of 'apparent death' and 'real death'). Man must respect the moment of rupture between soul and body. This rupture does not belong to him; he is subject to it. He must, of course, do all he can to preserve man's health, and maintain him in the blossoming of his human life; yet he must respect this ultimate moment which remains enigmatic for those who look at it from without. For the contemplative philosopher, death is the moment when the spiritual soul returns to its source, to its Father. Is this not the greatest moment in human life, the moment when the soul separates itself from the body in order to be alone in the presence of the One who is its Creator? This passage from the 'worldly' milieu to this purely personal and spiritual relation is great and most astonishing. Many people today, influenced by a positivist mindset, only consider death externally and no longer know how to respect it. Their capacity for admiration seems to stop with admiration for scientific and technical progress, while the inventors themselves seem to be accorded less respect. Is this not a type of idolatry? After rejecting God from their conscience, many people forget man's dignity and no longer admire anything but the visible work that he has realized (whether it be a work of art or a tool is of little importance). This is the tragedy of Western culture. Efficiency has become so impressive that it seeks to dominate everything. Is not 'modern' man in the process of blindly opting for efficiency – whatever form it takes – forgetting and even rejecting fruitfulness? If woman is the source of life in and through her maternity, she is indeed a great symbol of fruitfulness; and if the 'dragon' is a symbol of power and efficiency, one understands the great vision of the book of Revelation from the Bible: the woman about to give birth and the dragon standing before her, waiting, seeking to devour her progeny.[8] This has always been the struggle in every culture, yet in today's Western world it has taken on a unique dimension, blatantly manifesting itself. Love, in its deepest, most spiritual aspect, is forgotten. Is not love what philosophers have most 'forgotten' to consider attentively? For this reason, philosophy has been progressively reduced to technique, or methodology – that is, formal logic or analysis of language. Man, in his true dimension as able to love, adore, and contemplate, is no longer acknowledged; he is without rights. Indeed, man is beyond formal logic and the analysis of language. The proper value of formal logic and analytical philosophy is as instruments at the service of thought and contemplation. When they are considered in themselves as the only reality, what ensues is an exaltation of the tool, the instrument, for itself; man, the source of the instrument, is forgotten. Forgetting love leads to forgetting man and exalting the tool. The exaltation of the tool leads to the exaltation of pure efficiency.

The philosopher's role is to remind man that he lives in fierce combat, for his human dignity is at stake. When the combat reaches its

8 Rev. 12:1–4.

paroxysm, hope is always greatest and most intense. Man, in his depths, cannot be destroyed. Man can be imprisoned and alienated, every visible exercise of his freedom can be suppressed, his life imperiled or even destroyed, but what is noblest in him – his spiritual soul – escapes this. In certain circumstances he may even experience, at these moments, great freedom: that of adoring, contemplating, and also loving interiorly his fellow human beings – since all other activities have been rendered impossible. At such moments of acute crisis, under the weight of the greatest tyranny, man can discover what is deepest in himself, and can even offer himself for all those who reject it. Socrates comes to mind and, in a different way, Jesus Christ; and, following them, all those who accepted being thrown into prison, dying in order to be faithful to what is greatest in man, that is, the search for truth and love.

10

CRITICAL REFLECTION

We have gone through the major stages of philosophical inquiry. We have simply put them in context and purposely not considered them at length. From experience which implies the judgment of existence, we have moved on to a contemplative 'gaze' which considers everything in a new light and requires us to return to all that was previously considered in order to deepen it further. This shows that a philosophy which is ended and brought to completion in contemplation can be neither systematic nor dialectic, for it proclaims the primacy of spiritual love and is completely ordered to man's happiness. Now we must show how philosophy must have a reflective and critical outlook on its own development. All philosophy of that-which-is considered from the viewpoint of being, becoming, life, must also include reflection on the development proper to the intellect. This reflective attitude, while secondary, is nevertheless essential. It will help us to understand better the fragility of the mind and its extremely complex conditioning – which explains why there is such diversity among philosophical paths. It will also help us to understand better the nobility of the mind, its capacity to attain to truth. This part of philosophy should assume what is true in the philosophical perspective known as 'philosophy of the spirit, or mind' – which affirms the primacy of the consciousness of thought.

As soon as we reflect upon intellectual development, we notice its extreme diversity. What is interiorly lived (*vécu*) in one's knowledge is extremely varied and often complex. This is the first observation to be made, and it is denied by no one. Philosophical positions begin to vary, however, with the hierarchical order discovered in this *vécu*.

We can immediately discover various areas, or zones, of reflection in the *vécu* of our knowledge. There are the zones reached by our various sensations, our imagination, our memories, our capacity for reflection and meditation, our affective knowledge, our poetic and artistic knowledge, and our very discernment of this diversity. Our reflection is able to stop at the sense of touch, sight, hearing ... I hear a particular voice and can be completely attentive to it. I see such-and-such a color and can be wholly attentive to it as well. Our reflection can get caught up in the play of our imaginative representations. We can live in a very rich, very fluid imaginary world, a world that we can also enrich with memories. Our reflection can go beyond the world of imaginative representation, seek to discover our affective knowledge, and dwell on it. We can know when loving and love when knowing, as happens when we are in the presence of a loved one who loves us and speaks to us. Our reflection can discover within imaginative representation a particular type of knowledge, i.e., poetic and artistic knowledge. This type of knowledge inclines us to realize, express and say what it bears. Our reflection can also analyze the development of our intellect in the various sciences, mathematics, and philosophy. There is then something new; we go beyond the realm of imaginative representation to enter into that of meaning and truth sought for its own sake.

This last area of reflection possesses much greater lucidity than the preceding ones, for it considers the development of our intellectual life itself. The other areas of reflection are only possible because of it. We might say that the life of the intellect in itself implies consciousness and 'self-lucidity,' whereas sensations in themselves do not. It is due to the ascendency of the intellect over the sensations that the latter become conscious and we can reflect upon them. This is also true of the imagination and, in a completely different way, affective and poetic knowledge, for these types of knowledge involve the intellect. These are all the possible alliances between our intellect and our various powers, with a view to the full blossoming of our human life. The intellect is capable of irradiating these types of knowledge and the sensible and spiritual appetites.

In a critical reflective approach, we start by reflecting upon the core of the intellectual life, that which enables all the other areas of our human life to become lucid and conscious.

The core of the intellectual life entails a certain diversity. Nevertheless, we can analyze it fairly quickly and discover what is most central. Scientific development, important as it may be, is clearly not primary and essential in our intellectual life. It is a considerable enrichment, but only an enrichment. It is not the primordial source, for scientific development is reasoning. It is inquiry at various levels. Now, this reasoning, however essential to our intellectual life, is complex. It cannot be the core of the life of the intellect. At the starting point and the end of such reasoning, there are judgments expressed as propositions. These may be the core of the intellectual life. They are certainly diverse, yet in themselves they have a certain unity, a certain indivisibility. They are the first moment in which the intellect thinks affirmatively or negatively. Is this not the first lucid moment of the intellect? It is the core to which we must always return. It is on these judgments that critical reflection must primarily focus. Yet we must also be attentive to the fact that this core may not be what is most primitive in the life of the intellect, for our judgments are immediately varied, affirmative and negative judgments. There is a duality in this core which indicates that there is something simpler: the first hidden, enveloped moment of the life of the intellect, an embryonic moment which can only be the grasp of forms and determinations. The intellect, in the first moment of its life, apprehends that which is immediately its good, that which it is capable of assimilating.

Moreover, we should note that language indicates this to us; the simplest judgment is the judgment which affirms 'this is.' This judgment is enunciated in a composition and is, therefore, not absolutely simple. It unites two elements which pre-exist in our intellect: the 'this' and the 'is'; the noun which indicates something ('this') and the verb ('is') which indicates the fact of existing.

THE ELEMENTARY OPERATION OF THE INTELLECT (APPREHENSION)

If we are to unveil the first hidden moment of our intellectual life, we must reflect upon the intellectual act by which the form (the *to ti en einai*) of reality is apprehended.[1] This act never exists alone, separately, in a pure state. It only exists in a judgment, just as an element never exists in a pure, unmixed state, and love of a good never exists without desire and an intention. Nevertheless it has its own specification, its proper structure which we must analyze if we are to penetrate the life of the intellect. If we do not analyze it, like Ockham we often replace it with an intellectual intuition and no longer understand what the judgment of existence is in all its purity. Indeed, we must not forget that the slightest deviation at the source has immense consequences for the conclusion.[2]

The elementary operation of the intellect apprehends. It grasps the determinations of reality. Upon grasping them the intellect assimilates them. It carries them within itself and conceives them. In this assimilation the intellect is receptive to these forms. It is determined,

1 See above, p. 82 note 10.
2 Cf. Aristotle, *De Caelo*, I, 271 b 8–13.

specified by them. At the same time it is active, for by assimilating them, it transforms them. It gives them a new mode which we call 'intentional': the intellect destroys nothing of these realities in assimilating their determinations, yet it is determined by these forms and, in conceiving them, determines itself. Unlike the assimilation of the vegetative life, where the food is destroyed in order to be assimilated, the assimilation of the form of existent reality does not involve the destruction of the reality. That is why we call the assimilation 'intentional,' to show that it occurs in complete dependence upon the known reality's form without existentially altering it. A new form of reality appears with knowledge, especially with intellectual knowledge.

In order to explain how this intentional assimilation occurs, we are obliged to posit an 'intentional form' at its starting point and an 'intentional form' at its term. This intentional assimilation, which occurs in the intimacy of the intellect, requires that the intellect is determined at the starting point by an intentional form which permits it to assimilate this form (the former 'becomes' the latter). In this sense we can say that the intellect carries this first form within itself (we shall later specify where this form comes from: is it innate or does it arise from experience?) and that, reacting vitally and intellectually, it assimilates the form and conceives it. The intellectually known and assimilated form is called a 'concept' (a *verbum*, as the medieval scholastics used to say). A concept has meaning. It signifies the form of the reality inasmuch as it is intellectually grasped or known. It is important to underscore that this is the first moment of signification, or meaning.[3] It is the first awakening of the life of the intellect, its first 'fruit.' But to explain this 'concept,' the fruit of an act of intentional assimilation realized in the inmost life of the intellect, the former needs to have been anteriorly determined, specified by an intentional form. Now the image of an experienced reality, formed within our imagination, cannot perform this function, for it remains at the level of sensible intentionality. It is an image which represents a sensed reality, but

---

3 Our language, our words, only have meaning to the degree that they 'symbolically' refer to our concepts. We see the difference between this position and certain modern systems – analytical philosophy in particular – which are, moreover, directly dependent upon positivist philosophy. The positivist attitude, which refuses to return from the effect to the true cause and which mistakes the cause and the *sine qua non* condition, comes to consider the effect no longer as effect but as a reality in itself and relative only to its *sine qua non* condition (the antecedent). In the present case, positivism no longer considers the word relative to its cause (the signifying concept) but only its function within the sentence.

it is not the form of the reality as it is thought. Thus we must posit a pure active light in the intellect, capable of illuminating the sensible image (the 'phantasm') and extracting from it an intentional form. Every act of the intellect presupposes an internal illumination which transforms the 'phantasm' into an 'intentional form.' We have no immediate awareness of this, yet we posit it in order to explain this transformation of a phantasm, a transformation which allows it to cooperate with the intellectual life and whose term is this assimilation, this 'intentional conception.' This 'illumination' is the work of what is called the 'agent' or 'active intellect,' which, according to Aristotle, is like a light.[4]

With these considerations we specify the vital role of the intellect, its spiritual superiority over the imagination and the senses, and, at the same time, its receptivity to the realities it knows. In knowing physical reality, the intellect is transformed by it. The intellect also transforms its form, its determination in assimilating it. It transforms the form by giving it a new way of existing, which it does by interiorly illuminating it, starting from images. It is also transformed by this form; it is determined by it, carries it in its inmost self, and conceives it.

The action of the active intellect, this illumination, occurs within a certain abstraction. All spiritual illumination involves abstraction: while it illumines certain essential determinations it leaves other aspects in the dark; it both highlights and casts shadows. We can see an analogy with nutritive assimilation, for the latter also occurs by process of selection, by rejecting certain toxic or unassimilable elements.

This is how we discover the embryonic core of intellectual life, the source of an intimate fruit: a concept. This concept is, therefore, inseparable from our intellectual life; the former 'adheres' to the latter while being distinguished from it, like the pearl to the shell. A concept is this first instant when the intellect is intentionally 'one' with that which it knows. We must not, however, confuse a concept with what Descartes called 'idea.' This idea is known in and by itself. An idea is of the order of possibles (in fact, it is the fruit of inspiration, of intuition), whereas a concept is not known in and by itself. We unveil a concept in analyzing the first instant of the intellectual life, but we are not conscious of it. It is preconscious. So, today, when some, such as Heidegger, speak of 'pre-conceptual' knowledge, it is, in fact, 'preconscious' knowledge and not knowledge prior to concept, the intimate and hidden fruit of our intellectual life. With Descartes, a basic

4 Cf. Aristotle, *On the Soul*, III, 5, 430 a 14–16.

concept, the fruit of apprehension, is transformed into 'idea,' the fruit of intuition; for with Descartes the intuition of the *cogito* is primary.

This first moment of the life of the intellect, while simple, is not always the same. It is disclosed in our judgments, which are varied. These judgments are affirmative or negative: judgments of existence, judgments expressing a principle, hypothetical judgments, scientific judgments, etc. Apprehension, therefore, occurs at very diverse levels. We can point out two extremes: a first, very imprecise, very vague, judgment; and a judgment discovering the ultimate principle of metaphysics: being-in-act. We can thus specify that the first apprehension according to the genetic order is of a 'confused' whole, and that the ultimate apprehension is of act in so far as we can grasp its intelligible content, a content which is beyond all quiddity – the first grasped forms and the ultimate intelligible content; between the two are all the other forms (what have been called the 'categories').

Yet we must understand that these forms, these determinations, are grasped in a way completely different from the Kantian forms. For Kant they are a matter of a priori forms which understanding can consider in themselves, independent of existent reality. Is this not the critical foundation for Descartes' ideas? These a priori innate forms determine our understanding before any other knowledge does. This is a strong affirmation of the primacy of the knowing subject as the formal measure of knowledge. In this perspective there is no true objective knowledge. Kant's critique of speculative knowledge does not go far enough, for he no longer distinguishes between the spiritual primacy of the mind in its exercise of illumination and its receptivity to the objective determinations of known reality. This lack of distinction obliges him, in order to safeguard the primacy of the mind, to posit a priori forms and, in the end, transcendental subjectivity. Consequently, the object can no longer be that which primarily specifies the act of apprehension. It can no longer be anything but the experienced reality, the known reality. This is a materialization of the object's proper role. Intellectual knowledge is analyzed in the same way as physical becoming or a work of art, by distinguishing between matter and form. The analysis of intellectual knowledge, however, can only be undertaken at the level of being by distinguishing that-which-is in the act of being and its quiddity.

No deduction can be made from this critical analysis of apprehension because this analysis is, in fact, a reductive approach, the purpose of which is to unveil the *element* of our intellectual life. Hence we must now consider judgment, the perfect act of our intellectual life, of whose operation we are conscious. We shall then compare these two operations in order to grasp their deep connection.

PERFECT OPERATION OF THE INTELLECT (JUDGMENT)

The first fundamental judgment is that which concerns existent reality
and answers the question, 'Does this exist?' Our intellect answers, 'This
is.' This affirmative judgment is primary. It is prior to the negative
judgment, 'This is not.' A very simple sign of this anteriority is given
to us in language: the negation adds something to the affirmation; the
former therefore presupposes the latter. Yet beyond the sign, we must
specify that the affirmative judgment is indeed first, because it is the
simplest and most perfect of our judgments and the negative judgment
really presupposes it. The negative judgment could not be understood
if it were first; it is always in reference to the affirmative judgment. The
affirmative judgment is an act of the intellect which adheres to that-
which-is, which acknowledges that-which-is. This act is conscious; it
implies self-lucidity, a discernment. This act can assert that it is true,
in other words, that it conforms to that-which-is. This is its perfection.
We can affirm: 'What I say is true.' In affirming this, we are capable of
discerning that what has been grasped in existent reality and intellectually conceived in the inmost intellect, corresponds to existent reality;
it is really like this, the reality exists as has been stated. It is clearly in
the affirmation, the simplest affirmation ('this is'), that we most
immediately discover these various elements; whereas in the negation
('this is not') there is no longer adhesion, although there can still be
truth, for I can say, 'It is true that this is not.' This truth consists in
affirming that 'this' (that is to say, the content of our knowledge with
respect to a particular reality) does not exist, and thus rejecting it.
Negation makes use of affirmation in order to show its truth.

   Note, however, that negation possesses something very particular. It
is the pure fruit of our intellect. It does not exist in reality. Thus with
negation I grasp the superiority of my intellect, its capacity to draw
back, to distance itself in a very particular manner, to withdraw. The
imagination and sensations do not negate; they can suspend their
exercise, but they cannot negate. This ability is proper to the intellect;
that is why the transcendental superiority of a thinking subject is
primarily expressed in negation. It is, moreover, the only thing which
is positively expressed, for we acknowledge in absolute negation – 'this
is not' – that a reality does not exist. We see how one can readily
consider negation as liberating the intellect from its dependence upon
existent reality and allowing it to be perfectly itself. Is this not the
cause, in so far as we consider the primacy of a thinking subject over
known reality, of progressively asserting the primacy of negation over
affirmation? In order to liberate the intellect from its dependence upon

that which is known, we assert the primacy of negation. Hence, in this perspective, everything must start with negation. Negation allows us to live dialectically, to live the mind's deep becoming. It is what allows us to discover being. Heidegger did refuse to identify negation with Nothingness, which allows Being to be unveiled and made present; but in reality 'Nothingness' can have a positive action and unveil Being only if it is identical to negation as in the Hegelian dialectic. Heidegger would like to have liberated himself from it in order to rediscover a 'fundamental' ontology through Nothingness distinct from negation, yet this is the ultimate aspect of transcendental subjectivity: beyond negation there is *ontic* Nothingness which renders Being present.

The simplest judgment is indeed an affirmative judgment, which is also the most perfect. Among affirmative judgments, the simplest is the judgment of existence, the one which enunciates, 'this is.' Through the judgment of existence, the intellect acknowledges the primacy of that-which-is over what it enunciates, for that-which-is is the measure of what the intellect enunciates. In order to be able to acknowledge the primacy of that-which-is over what is enunciated, the intellect must truly attain to that-which-is as that which is beyond what it possesses in its inmost self, its enunciation, the 'complex concept' which it forms in judging and expresses in the terms: 'this is.' Here we discover the fundamental realism of the intellect and the foundation of the whole of realistic philosophy. For if the intellect, in its basic judgment, were to remain at the level of 'complex concept,' of enunciation, without truly attaining to an existent reality distinct from its judgment, then all knowledge would remain at the level of intentionality; it would never get beyond it. Philosophy would, therefore, also be at this level; it would never be able to attain to existent reality. It would only be able to attain to 'intentional forms' and determine their various relations at this level. Thus it would remain at a dialectical level.

The intellect, when affirming 'this is,' and even when specifying 'it is true that this is,' touches that-which-is; it attains to the act of being of the 'this.' It acknowledges it. It is conscious of it. The intellect also acknowledges that it cannot assimilate it, it cannot apprehend it: this act of being is beyond what it apprehends. That-which-is transcends all quidditative forms, all categories. The intellect, in judging, in affirming, has a mode of knowledge which is no longer the elementary mode of assimilation. It adheres to and touches that-which-is, acknowledging that it is 'other' than what it knows about it, what it has grasped of it. It also acknowledges that what it has grasped of it is true, that it conforms to the existent reality; and that its knowledge is therefore not far from the existent reality. It acknowledges (without identifying itself with it) that its knowledge does not disfigure the existent reality, while not, however, being totally reduced to it. Its knowledge is not existent reality in the strong sense. It is relative to it; yet it is capable of saying it as it is.

This 'touching' of existent reality is what characterizes the judgment of existence and differentiates it from apprehension. While the latter enables us to discover the specifying object of our intellectual life in its first embryonic moment, the judgment of existence unveils to us that our intellect is capable of attaining to that-which-is, that it is completely ordered to being in its most proper aspect: its act of being. Judgment reveals that the intellect is not enclosed in the form, the quiddity of existent reality. Can we say then that the intellect, through the judgment of existence, discovers that its ultimate object is not form (the quiddity of existent reality) but that-which-is, the act of being? Would it not be better to say that the object in the precise sense as that which determines and specifies our intellect, is the form, the quiddity; but that that-which-is attained in a judgment of existence, is what measures the content of our judgment? That to which the intellect is entirely ordered is no longer the object in the precise sense but an existent reality which transcends us. Yet to attain to it truly, the intellect must not remain only in the apprehended forms; it must also apprehend, to the degree that it can, the act of being, the ultimate moment of our apprehension. Through this apprehension, the intellect indeed possesses a concept of being, yet this concept of being remains analogical and very imperfect. Moreover, it must be surpassed in the judgment of existence which affirms that-which-is and truly attains to existent reality.

This is important to underscore. Suarez's metaphysics – which played such an important role in Scholasticism, down to Wolff and after – transformed Aristotle's first philosophy, the philosophy of that-which-is as being, into the metaphysics of the concept of being (seen already with Ockham). In such metaphysics, the concept of being is considered for its own sake and, from it, various modes of being are distinguished: the finite and infinite mode, substance, act, and the 'transcendentals.'

What Ockham and Suarez affirm implies something true. There is indeed a concept of being. But this concept is not primary, and first philosophy in its proper inquiry never stops at this concept. It always rests upon the judgment of existence. Moreover, it always implies the judgment of existence in act. It is only from a critical perspective, which seeks to specify this concept, that it is considered for its own sake. In a critical perspective, we affirm that there is a concept of being which is not univocal but analogical.[5] One can therefore never precisely determine its content. This concept helps us, in the end, to grasp, from a critical perspective, the unity of philosophy and all its richness. The concept of being implies in act, in an implicit manner, all the primary concepts traditionally called 'transcendentals.' The term means that they go beyond the particular modes of being (categories) and are convertible with the concept of being (i.e., they have the same extension and comprehension).[6]

It would also be interesting to note how, in Ockham's philosophy, the judgment of existence was transformed. He considers that beyond all judgment and apprehension there is an intuitive intellectual knowledge regarding the purely intelligible. This intuitive knowledge affirms: 'I know' (*intellego*) or 'I love Socrates.' It can, thanks to sensation, come into contact with existent reality and affirm that a particular reality exists. Ockham specifies that, in this affirmation, both the intellect and the

5 That is why the primary division of this concept cannot be the finite–infinite division.

6 Do not confuse this meaning of 'transcendental' with the Kantian 'transcendental' which designates an a priori determination in the order of knowledge prior to all that arises from experience. The term 'transcendental' therefore has a totally new meaning for Kant. From Thomas Aquinas' perspective, transcendental expresses a mode of universality. The notions of good and truth have a universal mode, such that we call them 'transcendentals.' The transcendental mode, therefore, has no meaning in itself. Precisely speaking, it is qualified as a logical 'being of reason.' In the Kantian perspective, the transcendental determines the 'I think' (*Ich denke*), which renders the transcendental possible and is thus, as it were, a *sine qua non* condition for it, precisely because the transcendental would not exist without the 'I think.' Here we indeed have an absolute primacy of the knowing subject over all specification from experienced realities and, consequently, a completely new signification of the object which is then necessarily reduced to the experienced reality. On the other hand, we clearly see the difference between the positions of Ockham and Kant. Ockham's 'I think' is again found here, but it is diminished by Kant's critical mind until it is reduced to a pure capacity for knowledge; all determination comes from the a priori form, the transcendental. But from where does this a priori form come? It is innate. The 'I think' allows it to emerge into consciousness. For Ockham there is a primacy of the exercise of thought which is luminous, intuitive; for Kant there is a primacy of the possible in the exercise. But how is the possible to be understood in the 'I think'? Is it not by starting from the fundamental structure of physical, scientific thought that we are able to understand it? Is it not analogous to a hypothesis, which remains a possibility in thought and is indeed the basis of scientific research? A priori forms themselves would be analogous to mathematical axioms. We then better understand Kant's deep intention: to undertake a critique of metaphysical knowledge based upon a model of scientific knowledge (perhaps, we should say, even more deeply: based upon a model of artistic knowledge). But did Kant truly attain to the speculative knowledge which he sought to criticize?

sensations attain to existent reality. As a matter of fact, the intellect, through the sensations, acknowledges that an existent reality is present. Consequently, the intellect no longer touches that-which-is in the judgment of existence. It simply acknowledges that a reality is there, present, that it exists for me. The judgment of existence is then expressed in the following manner: 'there is a particular reality there'; and no longer: 'this reality exists.' We see how the intellect, instead of making use of the sensations (while going beyond them) to attain to that-which-is and affirm that it exists, cooperates with the sensations without going beyond them, affirming precisely what they grasp. The intellect then no longer truly 'touches' that-which-is.

Given the importance of the judgment of existence for realistic philosophy, we can understand how, as soon as it is set aside (as in phenomenology or in knowledge pertaining to the physical, biological, or social sciences), we remain inevitably enclosed in the realm of intentionality and no longer come into contact with that-which-is. Such intellectual development can be interesting and profitable, but it does not allow contact with existent reality, with that-which-is. For we can only grasp reality and analyze it if it is at the starting point. Otherwise, it can never be met. Existent reality, that-which-is, cannot be met through the intentional, however spiritual the intentional might be. The intentional comes from existent reality and is totally relative to it. As soon as we consider it for itself, it veils reality and no longer leads us to it, for it is not of the same order. Such is the tragedy of phenomenology that seeks to rediscover reality. Starting from intentional forms, from ideas, it can never meet forgotten reality.

We cannot stop at the judgment of existence. It is a starting point. Thereafter come judgments enunciating the proper principles of philosophy; for example, the judgment which affirms, 'Substance is the principle and the cause, in the order of determinations, of that-which-is.' While this judgment does imply an adherence to that-which-is, it is primarily intellectual knowledge, acquired by induction, of a proper principle of that-which-is. Such a judgment possesses an essential unity, for it grasps an indivisible principle, a proper cause of that-which-is. Consequently, it has a necessary character, for that which is grasped (the connection between the predicate and the subject) imposes itself with evidence. Such a judgment can be true and can possess awareness of truth. However, what measures the content of the intellectual affirmation is not directly existent reality, but what is reached in existent reality by the intellect, thanks to an induction. What is reached cannot be pointed at visibly. Hence there is no direct verification. This is what makes the character of this judgment so particular. It imposes itself upon the intellect of those who have discovered it, but not directly or immediately upon those who hear it enunciated. The latter must make the same inductive discovery for themselves. Otherwise, they will receive the principle based on authority, and thus as an opinion.

This principle remains veiled by the existent reality. It is indeed radically in the reality, but formally, as a principle only, in the intellect of the one who discovers it. In this respect we grasp the difficulty for philosophical instruction and how such instruction always risks transforming philosophy into dialectic, for the discovery of proper principles can only be personal: it cannot be transmitted.

Let us not forget that, in this particular judgment, the grasp of proper principles always remains concurrent to or in continuity with the judgment of existence The latter is not laid aside; it is present. This grasp is the fruit of an induction which rests directly upon our experiences involving a judgment of existence, a direct contact with that-which-is. Nevertheless, the judgment implying this grasp penetrates into the heart of that-which-is by analyzing it, seeking its proper causes, by seeking that which is essential and primary in it (its determination, end, origin, and matter). This judgment makes us enter thereby into properly philosophical knowledge. The judgment of existence is only at its threshold. Properly philosophical knowledge cannot stop at a simple description of that-which-is, however useful and exhilarating this may be. It must analyze that-which-is (in the end, existent man) in the most penetrating manner possible, in order to discover its principles and causes. This must be done starting from our various experiences (work, friendship, cooperation, the experience of that-which-is-moved, the living being, that-which-is).

It would be interesting to examine here what differentiates this philosophical judgment from the judgment of a mathematician or a scientist who enunciates axioms, hypotheses, and laws. Let us at least note that philosophical judgment cannot abstract itself from the judgment of existence, whereas that of the mathematician and the scientist remains in a relation, a rapport. What the latter seek is a relationship of constancy between consequent and antecedent. This relationship is based upon a principle, a cause, but the principle or cause is not explicitly grasped by the scientist. A scientist grasps only one of its consequences – without specifying if the constant stems from one particular causality or another (such a specification has no meaning for the scientist; it is not what he is looking for). This explains the character of necessary relativity which envelops scientific research: one can always go further. The necessity is proper to a particular moment of research; but it can always be called into question.

The grasp of a proper principle should allow us to make a (philosophical) scientific judgment affirming a necessary connection between a particular quality and a particular reality. We then acknowledge that a quality is a property of a reality, that such-and-such reality cannot be without such-and-such quality. For example, when a philosopher states that one is the property of that-which-is, we have a scientific judgment, the content of which is a scientific conclusion. The truth of this judgment is its conformity with the proper principles upon which it depends. This truth is therefore not directly but mediately measured by that-which-is; it is nevertheless measured by that-which-is, for this judgment does not abstract itself from that-which-is. A scientific conclusion is the fruit of a demonstration, and demonstration presupposes the grasp of proper principles. We could, if we so desired, compare philosophical conclusions with the conclusions of the mathematical sciences, and make remarks analogous to those previously made regarding proper principles and scientific hypotheses.

It still remains to analyze the difference between (philosophical) scientific judgment and the judgment of wisdom made in the light of the first, creative causality. The judgment of wisdom is theological and proper to philosophy in its ultimate inquiry. This sapiential judgment explicitly entails a new judgment of existence. The only way we can speak of the First Being is to affirm that he exists, for we have no 'idea' about him, no 'concept' proper to him. We can only affirm that he exists and thereby negatively discover his manner of existing: He is without composition, absolutely simple; he is without potentiality, absolutely perfect, Pure Act. If the first judgment of existence – 'this is' – is transformed into 'a reality is present there,' if 'is' is no longer directly reached, and if 'being there' only signifies that which is 'situated there' beyond my knowledge, we can no longer discover the existence of a First Being. In order to say that here is a 'being,' an 'existing,' our sensations must necessarily detect it and touch it, which they cannot do for the existence of the First Being. Consequently, all philosophical content is reduced to quidditative content, that of ideas (of concepts–ideas) which can tell us nothing about the First Being.

The intellect however can discover the existence of the First Being and the causality between this First Being and other existent realities – including ourselves. The judgment of wisdom is made in the light of this connection of 'existential' causality. The judgment of wisdom therefore implies directly and eminently a judgment of existence. This judgment of existence is entirely other than the first ('this is'), yet it is wholly based upon the first judgment. If the first judgment is altered or set aside, one can no longer discover the existence of the First Being and the judgment of wisdom no longer has meaning. Having reduced the judgment of existence to 'an existent reality is present there,' analytical philosophy is consistent with itself when it claims that a judgment which discovers the existence of the First Being is totally devoid of meaning. Analytical philosophy depends upon Ockham's nominalism. It does not go far enough in its critique and does not rediscover the true meaning of the judgment of existence, 'this is.' It is regarding this that our critique must primarily be made.

Judgment can take on still another form when expressed as hypothesis. The possible then precedes, or comes before, that-which-is, before the act of being. From a philosophical viewpoint we discern two different levels in hypothetical judgment. First, the possible simply precedes that-which-is without excluding it; that-which-is is then not directly considered. Second, the possible is considered for itself and that-which-is is laid aside; the possible then not only surpasses but replaces that-which-is.

The first of these two hypothetical judgments has its place in realistic philosophy for research purposes. The second is outside realistic philosophy. It must be acknowledged that our intellect can readily remain at this latter level and be content there, for there it finds itself in the presence of pure intelligibles connatural to its proper way of knowing. Such judgments are a sort of prolongation of apprehension and become 'intuition' after the manner of Ockham. We are in the presence of a play of relations of opposition or of synthesis of 'ideas.'

At this level, truth is only a matter of internal coherence, of pure relations which correspond or are in opposition. We can no longer even speak of contradiction, for we are in a realm that contradiction does not penetrate (the major opposition is that of contrariety). Contradiction reaches that-which-is. Here we are in the realm of pure possibles.

Here we should distinguish various levels of possibles: logical and mathematical possibles, possibles at the level of artistic inspiration, possibles at the metaphysical level. Logical and mathematical possibles are the only ones which can be considered for themselves and in themselves.

Lastly, let us simply situate affective judgment and prudential judgment, poetic judgment and artistic judgment. Each of these judgments has a character which is irreducible to the others, showing the alliance of intellect with spiritual appetite in spiritual love, with creative imagination in inspiration, and with the *habitus* of prudence and art. In each case there is a different mode, or type, of truth. Note that with affective judgment, love specifies and determines intellectual knowledge. This judgment, however, is not absolute subjectivity. Rather, spiritual love grants us a new understanding of the one we love. We no longer know him or her from without as the 'other,' but from within. This gaze, or perspective, is objective, but such objectivity is different from that of a metaphysical perspective. In order to know a human person in depth, such affective knowledge seems to allow us to go further than so-called objective scientific knowledge, for it enables us to grasp a human person in his capacity to love another human person and be actuated and completed by him. Nevertheless, because a human person possesses a capacity for this actuation and completion not only by another human person, a friend, but also by the contemplation of his God, his Creator, affective knowledge is not what is ultimate. It is surpassed by sapiential, metaphysical knowledge which alone enables one to attain to the human person in his ultimate dignity, that is, his capacity to order himself to God.

The greatness of realistic philosophy is its ability to acknowledge the unique character of affective knowledge and sapiential knowledge. We cannot approach the human person in the same way we approach a material reality. The spirit cannot be grasped from without, unlike the physical world. If we want to understand the spirit in its most proper aspect, we must grasp it from within, through love. Knowing a human person as we do a physical reality is not true objectivity. It is to forget that we cannot consider a physical reality and a human person in the same way. In order to say this, however, we must understand that knowledge of that-which-is as being is beyond the distinction between the sensible and the spiritual; otherwise we oppose them or reduce the second to the first.

We could say something similar concerning poetic judgment, which enables us to look at the physical world in a different way to that of a scientist. Here again, the objectivity of the latter judgment must not exclude the entirely different way in which the world is regarded and evaluated by the poet.

REASONING

After having reflected upon the richness of judgment, the perfect act of the intellect, we should consider the vast realm of reasoning in which we grasp the becoming of our intellectual life.

Judgment places us in the presence (with the judgment of existence) of that-which-is and makes us understand that our intellect is entirely ordered to being and, consequently, to the contemplation of the One who is perfectly Being, Pure Act. Reasoning, in all its forms, enables us to discover that our intellect has an astonishing capacity for progress, growth, and development. Becoming is, therefore, not foreign to it, and this becoming gives it a certain efficacy and fruitfulness.

The relationship we establish between judgment and reasoning has immense consequences for one's philosophical perspective. The relationship is analogous to that established between being and becoming. In realistic philosophy, becoming is considered dependent upon being – that-which-is-moved implies that-which-is – and true end is always beyond becoming. Becoming is a mode of that-which-is. Consequently, a judgment – which makes us attain to that-which-is and discover a finality, and allows us to discover the First Being and contemplate him – is necessarily the most perfect, and all reasoning is at the service of judgment.

On the other hand, in a philosophy which affirms the primacy and transcendence of the thinking subject over that-which-is, becoming progressively gains the upper hand over being and the activity of reasoning comes to be regarded as giving meaning to our judgments. Indeed, from the viewpoint of efficient causality, our judgments of the proper principles of that-which-is are the fruit of an induction; our scientific judgments are the fruit of a demonstration. Only the judgment of existence is prior; but because it is pre-philosophical, some claim that philosophy in its essential and proper aspect must acknowledge the primacy of reasoning over judgment. This allows us to understand how dialectic defines philosophy; the primacy of efficient causality necessarily leads to such an affirmation. Only final causality grasped at the level of being keeps us from affirming the primacy of dialectic and enables us to re-establish the importance of the judgment of existence. For although it is pre-philosophical, the judgment of existence is present to the whole of philosophy. End, at the level of that-which-is, cannot be grasped without a judgment of existence.

As soon as we set the judgment of existence aside, or transform it by removing its original character and placing the 'intuition' 'I think' or 'I love' ahead of it (as did Ockham), we are inevitably led to the exaltation of a Hegelian type of dialectical thought. We acknowledge the primacy of the intelligible, the possible, over that-which-is. Becoming then absorbs being. Being is not forgotten, but absorbed by becoming. And if we wish to highlight being without discovering it in its originality, starting from the judgment of existence – our intellect still enslaved to the dialectical method and its primary intuition ('I know,' *intelligo*) –

there is no way out other than using 'nothingness' to recreate being, and claim to think it in its native state. Such being, however, is obviously not being discovered by starting from that-which-is. It is Being born from poetic intuition. The 'Name' of Being is proclaimed more than the discovery, in existent realities, of that-which-is and the act of being.

The great seduction of Hegelian dialectic comes from its spiritual appearance and from the fact that it seems to imply a sort of spiritual fruitfulness that places us, as it were, beyond the physical world – without disdaining it, but absorbing it. In fact, Hegelian dialectic does not attain to the 'spiritual.' It attains to the spiritual intentionality of the *vécu* of our mind reflecting upon itself, affirming and negating. There is no true spiritual fruitfulness in dialectic but a sort of efficacy at the intentional level. True fruitfulness always comes from love. What is most terrible about this dialectic is that the mind becomes enslaved to itself and exalts itself. It remains in its own immanence. And as soon as we accept entry into dialectic, we can no longer leave: there is no exit, for the play of relations is so strong and so intense.

When we return to realistic philosophy we acknowledge that intellectual activity, at the level of becoming, has two great paths of development: induction and deduction. The inductive path is the discovery of proper principles, starting from experience and in the light of questioning (when one no longer questions, the intellect stops, the bow slackens). The inductive path makes our intellect progress and enables it to discover its proper good, that which structures it and gives it its rigor.

The deductive path is a way of making explicit the riches grasped in principles. It is no longer discovery in the proper sense. It is the ordered, organic deployment of all that is already possessed. That is why the intellect is so at ease in this realm. It becomes aware of the richness of what it possesses.

This type of deductive path has many variations: from first philosophy to rhetoric, from apologetics (entirely ordered to persuasion) to formal and rigorous mathematics.

We cannot stop at these scientific conclusions, however. They are an effect, a fruit of the intellectual life, not an end. One does not contemplate scientific conclusions. They are a stage, a stepping stone which enable us to advance further, a stage completely different in philosophy than in the modern sciences. For a philosopher, it is a stage on the way to the discovery and contemplation of the First Being. For a scientist, it is a stage on the way to progress in scientific research which, of itself, has no end other than its own continuous advancement.

Besides these two major paths there are others, in particular that which allows us to discover the First Being. This is a unique type of demonstration, for it does not, strictly speaking, end in a conclusion but in the existence of One who is First. It is not an induction, for it does not end in a proper principle but in an ultimate and primary Reality. Nevertheless, this path contains something of these two elementary paths; it is much more complex and requires an ultimate effort of the intellect.

There is also the reductive path of the intellect, which is no longer the search for a principle, a property, or the ultimate Reality, but for its elementary aspect. It is the discovery of the element of our intellectual life or the physical universe. We are then in the order of 'how.'

Imaginative and Sensitive Knowledge

After this critical reflection on the deep structure of our intellectual life, we must examine the connections and the distinctions between our intellectual knowledge, our imaginative knowledge, and our sensible knowledge. The judgment of existence implies the cooperation of these three types of knowledge.

Imaginative knowledge remains at the level of sensible images ('icons') which represent, in us, the physical world. What characterizes the realm of representative images, the realm of sensible imaginary intentionality, is its perpetual becoming. Imaginative sensible intentionality comes from the sensations and develops according to its own demands, according to infinite associations. Nothing can stop nor limit the extension of these associations which have no other end than their own development. That is why this realm is essentially relative and in never-ending becoming.

The intellect can make use of these images in different ways. It can make use of them with a view to its own development; the active intellect illumines them and enables them to be at the origin of intentional intelligible forms. It can make use of them in another way by illuminating them, without extracting the intelligible forms from them, but remaining in them and transforming these images, formalizing them in a very particular way. This is what characterizes the development of mathematical intellect. Mathematical possibles are born from images. The intellect can also make use of these images by considering their connections with the passions and with sensations. This is how the poetic imagination develops. We are then in the presence of the 'possible' of artistic ideas, of symbols. Thus we see how three types of intelligible 'possibles' are born from images.

It would also be interesting to see the role which images play at the level of affective, spiritual, and sensible knowledge (the passions).

The imagination is the 'turntable,' the 'switchboard' for psychic development. It links us both to our instincts (through passions) and to our intellect (through intentional forms).

In the prolongation of the imagination, it is memory which preserves sensible images and organizes them. Through memory and imagination, our life of sensible knowledge has great autonomy and richness. It is a whole world of interior images that we carry, and a world that develops within us. This world of images can envelop us to the point of invading us, enclosing us within itself, and preventing us from going further. What should be at the service of our intellectual life, as 'matter' capable of being transformed into intelligible intentional forms under the illuminative action of the active intellect, can overwhelm us and bring our 'vision' to a halt. We then become enslaved to the incessant sparkling of images and remain in a feverish agitation that excites the passions, which should rather be at the service of the intellectual life and spiritual life. Imagination and memory can become their worst enemies.

Our various sensations – knowledge in its most fundamental and primitive aspect – place us in direct and immediate contact with the physical world, with the realities that we experience around us. Sensation is knowledge which, while remaining in contact with the physical world, possesses something that goes beyond the physical world and is proper to it. Through sight we 'become' certain sensible qualities – color, light – but without modifying them. We are modified in our senses by these sensible qualities. We intentionally 'become' them; we intentionally carry them within us. The physical organ can experience disturbances if these sensible qualities are too violent; such disturbances are certainly accidental, but they condition our sensations and can, if too violent, even hinder our sensations. What is certain is that, as regards sensations, we depend upon the presence of the physical realities affected with these qualities. When this presence disappears, sensation disappears, and it can only remain in our imagination and our memory. Our sensations are thus completely relative to the qualities of physical realities and the former must remain in contact with the latter in order to exist and be preserved.

Moreover, there is something unique in each of our external senses. Each is capable of knowing certain 'proper sensibles' which the others cannot sense. There are also other sensibles which are common to several senses. It is important to specify this in order to understand the originality of each sense and its privileged contact with physical reality, a contact which cannot be replaced by another sense. Sight knows light and color. Hearing knows sounds. Touch knows hot and cold, dryness and dampness ... On the other hand, magnitude, movement, number, figure can be grasped by sight, or sound, or touch. These 'common sensibles' are measurable, whereas the 'proper sensibles' are indivisible and, in their proper aspect, escape all measurement. Thus, with the proper sensibles, we better grasp what our sensations are. In knowing these proper sensibles through our senses, we first discover the qualities of existent physical realities. We are in direct contact with these realities through sensation. Thanks to such qualitative sensitive contact, our intellect can affirm that a particular reality exists.

The judgment of existence is the fruit of the alliance between our intellect and our external senses, especially that of touch; for among the senses touch is the most fundamental, the one that can separate itself from the others, yet the one the others always involve. The judgment of existence is the fruit *par excellence* of the intellect making use of touch, thereby affirming 'this is,' 'this warm reality exists.' Through this judgment the intellect grasps something other than what touch, in itself, grasps, for it affirms 'this *is*.' It 'touches' the existing, the existence, in the 'this.' Thus it makes use of touch in order to have this immediate qualitative contact, this actual contact, with the 'this' that is. If one sets the proper sensibles aside, claiming that they are not objective (as does Descartes), and only accepts the 'common sensibles,' the intellect can no longer have immediate contact with that-which-is. The 'common sensibles' belong to the realm of the measurable, quantity, the divisible. They are not what is ultimate, what is in act in existent physical reality. Consequently, the intellect no longer affirms 'this is,' 'this is in act of being'; it simply acknowledges an existent datum, exterior to itself, situated beyond itself, present. The common sensibles do not manifest the act of being at the sensible level. They show the connection, the relation between a particular individual reality and the whole. They show the individual character of a particular physical reality, distinct and separated from the others, but they do not manifest what is most actual in it (its proper qualities), and thus do not manifest its act of being.

It would be interesting to grasp the relation between the five contacts we have with physical reality, in and through our various senses, and the five fundamental questions of the intellectual life. These five questions cannot be given in an a priori way; they must necessarily come from our experience. Indeed, our intellect can only be determined by experience. The primary, fundamental determinations, the ones which are, as it were, the first 'pleats', or 'grooves' of the intellectual life, can only come from our most characteristic experiences. Examining the connections between the sensation present in the different judgments of existence and subsequent questions helps us to understand that our questions disclose what is proper to a spirit bound to a body or, if one prefers, to an intellect dependent upon sensations.

Some of these connections are clear; others are more difficult to detect. What is certain is that our fundamental experience of the physical world comes about through the intermediary of touch and on account of touch. Consequently, the intellect finds itself conditioned in a fundamental way. It then asks, 'Out of what?' or 'In what?,' which leads to the discovery of material cause. Through sight, the intellect has a completely different contact with physical reality and it finds itself conditioned in a completely different way, which leads to a new question, 'What is it?' Through hearing, the intellect is conditioned in yet another way, leading to the question, 'Whence does it come?' Here we can only suggest, while pointing out that there is a very important question here, which helps us to grasp the structure of the conditioning of our intellectual life.

Note, also, that the intellect, inasmuch as it is conditioned in its development by images, is led to ask 'how.' But here we can only pose questions and seek to indicate a true solution.

11

LOGIC

Close to critical reflection – but nevertheless distinct from it – is the question of logic. Logic was born with Aristotle and developed as an *organon*, an instrument of philosophical knowledge. We know (already with Ockham) that it progressively replaced metaphysical thought and was integrated as a normative part of philosophy. We also know that for many logicians today, formal logic constitutes true philosophy, everything outside of formal logic being considered 'sentiment.'

We cannot study the evolution of logic here, interesting as it might be. We shall just point out the problem as an important one for the twentieth- and twenty-first-century philosopher. This problem can only be truly analyzed, however, by considering the relationships between philosophical thought and mathematics on the one hand, and Aristotle's logic and formal mathematical logic on the other. When examining these relationships, we notice that, while the judgment of existence is the basis of Aristotle's philosophy and so of his logic (his philosophy is the basis of his logic), this judgment is set aside in mathematics and modern formal logic. There is no longer immediate or mediate reference to that-which-is. We are in the realm of possibles or, more exactly, of possible relations considered for themselves.

The proper of logical reflection – at least of Aristotelian inspiration – is the consideration of the mode which a known reality has in my intellect by the very fact that it is known. For example, by the very fact that I know Peter's nature, know his qualities and affirm that he exists, this nature, these qualities, and his being have, in my intellect, a particular manner of existing. This nature and these qualities exist in my knowledge with a universal mode, and this affirmed being exists in my judgment according to a new mode: it is 'attributed,' as a verb. The universal and the attribution do not exist in the existent reality which I experience, which I touch. They only exist in my intellectual knowledge, and I can only consider them by reflecting upon my proper knowledge of grasping and judging. We could make similar remarks regarding reasoning (inductive and demonstrative). The inference exercised in reasoning does not exist in the physical realities we experience. It only exists in our intellect which reasons. There is a sort

of 'transposition' from existent physical realities to intellectual knowledge which can be analyzed when we reflect upon how we grasp, judge,
and reason, and how reality – inasmuch as it is grasped and judged –
finds itself in our intellect. Thomas Aquinas, following Aristotle and
Avicenna, speaks of 'secondary intentions,' of 'beings of reason,' the
proper object of logic.

A 'being of reason' is a being which is, as it were, 'secreted' by our
intellectual knowledge, by our intellect. It is not 'natural' in the sense
that it is not of our physical universe. It is 'natural' in that it is not
artificial, that is, produced by art. It is not, in the proper sense, the
effect of a voluntary act, of artistic production. It is the 'fruit,' the
consequence, of a vital spiritual operation which is itself profoundly
natural. Like it or not, in knowing, my intellect abstracts and,
consequently, knows according to a universal mode. Clearly it is
possible for me not to stop at this proper manner of knowing. I can
ignore it and seek a primary intuitive knowledge beyond this abstract
mode (in the manner of Ockham or Bergson), yet even when I neglect
it, this abstract mode of knowing remains. My language is a manifest
sign of it, for the concrete words I employ have a capacity for
enveloping a multitude of individuals. I also make use of abstract
words, elaborated by reason from concrete words (whiteness comes from
white, *esse* comes from *ens*), and these abstract words possess a more
precise meaning, having abandoned certain material elements of the
meaning of the concrete words.

This 'being of reason' (universal, attribution, inference), is truly a
relation of reason, for it is neither substance, nor act, nor a quality.
There are no 'substances of reason,' nor acts of reason, nor qualities of
reason. Only a relation, owing to its feebleness, can be 'of reason'; in
other words, can be a relation directly based upon intellectual activity
and not in existent reality outside of the intellect.

That is why, although such reflection possesses a proper object (the
being of reason) which specifies knowledge of a special type, this
knowledge is not purely speculative knowledge. It is also artistic
knowledge ordained to realizing a work. For a being of reason always
involves various relations of reason capable of being united in various
ways in various syntheses, and capable of being opposed and divided.
One can, therefore, grasp the rules of these various syntheses and
divisions. Thomas Aquinas says that logic is the 'art of arts,' for it is
capable of directing our way of thinking.

We thereby see the difference between logic, critical reflection, and
philosophy. Realistic philosophy is always based upon existent reality,
upon the judgment of existence. Critical reflection seeks to explore the

realm of 'intentional forms'; it makes precise that which is grasped from intellectually known or sensed realities. As to logic, it considers 'beings of reason,' the way in which we know existent realities. As soon as we have understood what a 'being of reason' is, we can no longer accept dialectic as a philosophical method (whether it be Platonic dialectic or that of Hegel), precisely because this method no longer distinguishes reality in so far as it is known or grasped by our intellect, from reality in its proper manner of existing. That is why the dialectic which develops the becoming of our reason is considered to be what enables us to discover the becoming of existent reality in an absolute way. But is the becoming of reality and that of the living being dialectical? It does not seem to be so, for it is realized in a quantitative manner, with a certain juxtaposition and a certain exteriority – even if there is immanence. Dialectic claims to bring about unity beyond all opposition.

When we discover what a being of reason is, it is then easy to understand that logic implies:

  logic of the universal, corresponding to the embryonic grasp of our
    intellectual life;
  logic of attribution, based upon the judicative activity of our
    intellect; and finally,
  logic of inference, based upon the reasoning activity of our in-
    tellect.

Logic of the universal studies the classic problem of the 'predicables' – genus, specific difference, property, accident – and shows how we can define what we grasp. This need to define corresponds to an appetite for clarity. The intellect seeks to avoid confusion. Our intellect, in order to define, also makes use of division, because division removes confusion. Yet we cannot stop at this first type of knowledge which, while necessary, is very embryonic.

Logic of attribution considers how our enunciations, the fruit of our judgments, imply unity beyond the composition of noun and verb. This unity expresses the radical unity of that-which-is. The judgment of existence is indeed the foundation of all logic of attribution. In order to understand what attribution is, we must study what a noun is, what is a noun's proper function in the enunciation – which leads to the famous question of 'supposition.' A noun takes the place of the substantial reality for the communication of our thought, for saying. A noun is capable of receiving certain attributions.

We must also study what a verb is and what is its proper role. A verb expresses action. It is *par excellence* that which is attributed, that which supposes a subject, a noun, with which it is identified. In addition to the question of the oppositions of various enunciations, and the problem of the various ways in which attributions are made (categorical, hypothetical, and modal attributions), there is the question of composition and division.

Finally, logic of inference examines how our intellect is capable of passing from the diversity of sensible experiences to the discovery of a proper intelligible principle, a cause which can only be attained to by the intellect. This passage is what we call an induction. Yet we must clearly distinguish this type of induction from what Francis Bacon called 'induction.' The latter is typically quantitative; it is a type of generalization, whereas the induction of which we speak is qualitative. It involves a passage from the sensible many to a proper, indivisible principle. This passage is possible because the intellect, having grasped a certain unity in the diversity of determinations and qualities, questions to know the unity of determinations, the unity of orientations in the diversity of qualities. One in the diverse implies an order, which requires a principle. Because induction is a re-ascent to the source, to the principle, it always remains difficult. Very often we economize, i.e., avoid induction by being content with description. Only the discovery of a proper principle and a cause, however, enables the intellect to go further and grasp its proper good, that which truly specifies it. It is with the grasp of proper principles and proper causes that the intellect becomes philosophical.

In addition, logic of inference examines how our intellect is capable of deducing certain conclusions from premises or immediate propositions. Such is the question of the deductive syllogism, whose various forms we must consider. Through this we can understand the efficacy of the intellect.

When deductive reasoning is exercised with respect to something necessary – that is, starting from premises which are first and true proper principles – we have a demonstration, a source of scientific knowledge. When reasoning occurs in matters of opinion, we have knowledge which remains opinion, we have dialectical thought as Aristotle understood it. It is very important to distinguish clearly these different types of reasoning.

We cannot linger here on the discovery of the logical rules of demonstration and syllogism; but it was necessary to situate logic as an instrument of philosophical thought in order to understand better how our thinking (which begins with an intentional assimilation and thereby realizes a formal unity with existent realities, thanks to concept and through abstraction) becomes increasingly aware of its autonomy and originality. The development of our intellect occurs according to a rhythm and laws which are proper to it, which are not those of the growth of a living being only endowed with vegetative life; but such development remains analogous. In both cases growth and development involve becoming in a certain immanence. The latter of these developments cannot be perfect because of quantity; the former can be perfect, for it is realized beyond quantity. The latter is substantial, the former, intentional.

Thanks to its lucidity, the intellect discovers that it can neither become as does a physical reality – in itself it is beyond quantitative conditioning, beyond juxtaposition – nor develop according to the rhythm of vegetative life. We discover that the intellect can nonetheless develop and progress in complete autonomy, for in its vital exercise it always remains dependent upon existent reality. Thus there is an incessant confrontation between the exercise of our intellect and the becoming of physical realities and the growth and decline of living realities.

This confrontation is strongest in the judgment of existence. The intellect therein acknowledges both its independence and its dependence. This is the crucial place or moment in which we grasp the intentional unity realized within the life of the mind and its dependence upon existent reality. In reasoning, it discovers itself as autonomous, independent, as a source capable of developing in its own way; yet it also acknowledges in demonstration (the most perfect reasoning) that its true autonomy can never be separated from existent reality, and thus from the judgment of existence. The great temptation is to withdraw into one's own autonomy and to develop exclusively according to this autonomy. This is what characterizes Platonic and Hegelian dialectic.

Logical research and critical research remain reflective types of research. The philosopher can neither stop nor remain there, because such research has no other purpose than to help a philosopher to be more lucid and have a discourse which is more limpid and less confused, and which better expresses what he has grasped in reality.

These two types of research nevertheless have a priority in the order of consciousness and communication. That is why, when consciousness and communication are exalted, it is normal to reduce philosophical inquiry to such reflective research. The demands of truth, as well as the demands of contemplation, then tend to disappear.

EPILOGUE

At the end of this philosophical 'itinerary' it is easier to ascertain the richness proper to realistic philosophy. Realistic philosophy is indeed at the service of man's full development. It must enable him to discover his end, his purpose. Realistic philosophy must enable man to discover the depth of his spirit, that is, his capacity to love and choose another human person as friend and, even more profoundly, his capacity to discover, adore, and contemplate his Creator. Friendship and contemplation are the two great orientations of his will, his heart, and his intellect. Such is true happiness. Such is man's personal end. Yet this end cannot be immediately attained. Before attaining his end, the human person experiences a becoming, a progression realized within a certain conditioning. This conditioning consists of his familial and political communities, united and linked by the work community.

We can recognize the difficulty in asking: How do we harmonize end and becoming in man? It easily happens that, wishing to exalt end, we forget becoming, or that, only looking at becoming, we no longer discover end. We then either idealize or materialize and do not manage to get beyond the radical distinction between form and matter. This 'going beyond' can only occur with the discovery of that-which-is and its consideration from the viewpoint of being. Moreover, it is not surprising that idealistic philosophy as well as materialistic philosophy refuse metaphysics — for metaphysics can relativize them and show their error.

However, in order to discover metaphysical philosophy, philosophy which considers that-which-is, we must have discovered the originality of the judgment of existence, 'this is,' present in all our experiences. This judgment is precisely what took the longest to discover — think of the philosophical ascent preceding Aristotle[1] — and was most quickly forgotten, ignored, and rejected.

Our efforts must be directed to the discovery of the judgment of

1 With the Fathers of the Church and theologians who put philosophy at the service of faith, we find something analogous to the great philosophical discoveries of the Greeks. It was with Thomas Aquinas that the judgment of existence was made perfectly explicit; immediately after Thomas Aquinas, with Henry of Ghent, then with Duns Scotus, Ockham, and all of decadent scholasticism, the judgment of existence is no longer understood. As for the Thomistic renewal, has it truly rediscovered the judgment of existence?

170

existence if we wish to go beyond the opposition between idealism and materialism and rediscover man's true end – beyond his becoming, without disregarding his becoming.

INDEX

Made in the USA
Middletown, DE
27 January 2018